Also by Patricia Thorpe
The American Weekend Garden
Everlastings

Also by Eve Sonneman
Real Time
Roses Are Read

America's Cottage Gardens

America's Cottage Gardens

Imaginative Variations on the

Classic Garden Style

by Patricia Thorpe

Photographs by

Eve Sonneman

RANDOM HOUSE

NEW YORK

Dedication

For Matthew, Harry and Sam

Published in the United States by Random House, Inc., New York, and
simultaneously
in Canada by Random House of Canada Limited, Toronto.

Library of Congress Cataloging-in-Publication Data
Thorpe, Patricia.
America's cottage gardens: imaginative variations on the
classic garden style / by Patricia Thorpe and Eve Sonneman.
p. cm.
Includes index.
ISBN 0-394-56989-X
1. Cottage gardens, American.   I. Sonneman, Eve.   II. Title.
SB404.6.U5T46   1990
635.9—dc20   89-42777

Manufactured in Japan
98765432
First Edition

❧ Contents

The Northeast

America's Cottage Gardens

Introduction ❧ *What Is an American Cottage Garden?*

*f*orget for a moment any ideas you may already have about cottage gardens. Don't think of Gertrude Jekyll or Claude Monet, Margery Fish or Vita Sackville-West. Banish all thoughts of Giverny or Sissinghurst. Instead, think of the gardens you pass every day, the most familiar gardens around you, and the most remarkable. Remember the yards in your neighborhood that you may have loved as a child. Perhaps you had an aunt or grandmother who could always be found outside, clearing away leaves from early daffodils, sprinkling seeds for portulaca or alyssum, tying up the mums before the autumn storms. Maybe the man next door grew lettuce and corn and giant dahlias with flowers bigger than your head. These gardens don't exist only in our memories; they are still part of our day-to-day landscape in every part of America. They may be as picturesque as the roses and hollyhocks around a Nantucket saltbox; they may be as unexpected as fifteen thousand gladiolus on an eighth of an acre in Cody, Wyoming. They may be as humble as a rickety arbor of grapes and gourds amid basil and marigolds behind an Italian grocery store. But whether they are humble or picturesque, eccentric or outlandish, these are all American cottage gardens.

The term "cottage garden" has both advantages and drawbacks. It is impossible for some people to separate the term from the English garden tradition. True, this kind of garden making developed early in England (although we should remember its counterparts throughout Europe) to become during the eighteenth and nineteenth centuries a well-recognized and much imitated style. But the earliest cottage gardeners—farm workers, village craftsmen, anyone, really, with a small plot and a family to feed—were not intent on creating a recognizable tradition. They were simply learning to garden and trying to make the most of a little space. The little space was usually an eighth to a quarter of an acre and allowed for only the simplest design: A path to the front door was often the only organizing principle. The house was, of necessity, a focus of the garden.

Cosmos.
Cody, Wyoming, August.

Joe Ryan's tools.
Cooperstown,
New York, June.

The plots were invariably enclosed, and the walls of both house and garden were utilized as vertical growing space. The first cottage gardens concentrated on vegetables and fruit, herbs usually had a place, and easy, hardy decorative flowers filled up any gaps.

It was not until the nineteenth century that cottage gardening became so elevated a style. It was then that Romantic artists and other seekers of nostalgia began to present a greatly idealized version of the cottage garden to the public. It is not hard to understand the appeal of those gardens to the Romantic sensibility. They conveyed the perfect careless rapture so dear to that movement. Simple, naive and pretty, they were from a humble part of society and were dramatically different from the gardens being made by the upper class. But not for long. It soon became fashionable to create your own cottage garden—no matter if you were the master of thousands of acres. So cottage gardening in England, and in much of Europe with regional variations, began to appear in two forms: real cottage gardens, still, usually, the domain of the lower classes, eccentric and personal puttering by amateurs in the world of plants; and haute cottage gardens, the cleaned-up and well-financed version for the sophisticated and well-educated gardener, of which Giverny is probably the best-known example.

In America, there are elegant imitations of English cottage gardens, but they are not the concern of this book. What we are seeking across the United States are small yards created with much the same spirit that prompted the earliest English cottage gardeners, but usually created in complete ignorance of that tradition. It is no longer possible in England for a gardener to begin as if he had never seen a garden before; not only is it possible in America but it is usually the case. American cottage gardens end up having quite a bit in common with the English, but the differences are almost always greater than the similarities, and one of the greatest differences, not surprisingly, is the way they look.

*California spring. Laguna
Beach, California, April.*

It is possible that by using the term "cottage garden" in this book, we are inviting confusion with the English tradition. There is, however, no other succinct term by which to call small, personal, individual, eccentric, spontaneous gardens created by amateurs. So we will use the name, and try to outline here what it is that makes an American cottage garden.

The most obvious element of a cottage garden is its small size; its limited space has a definite effect on its appearance. The chief concern in a small space is getting a large number of plants in the ground. This results in plantings that use every inch of soil and produce what appears at first to be an abundant jumble of plants. Most cottage gardens are not really disorganized—they couldn't be and still make good use of their limited space. And they are seldom, if ever, messy. But they appear unruly because their organizing principles are not the ones to which we have become accustomed, especially if we are used to the formulas of border planting. A cottage plot is often ordered by very personal ideas, not always apparent to visitors. Even highly organized cottage gardens seldom look stiff because when everything is growing, you can scarcely see the ground. Cottage gardeners are not nervous about what colors go together or whether the short ones are in front of the tall ones. Elaborate design questions are usually not an issue; they are resolved by basic considerations like being able to get through the path. In general, American cottage gardens are larger than English models, and many have a more leisurely sprawl; their size and design are largely determined by the part of the country in which they are found.

Both American and English cottage gardens are created around the house or in close proximity to it, pushing up against the house and frequently climbing the walls. But America has few actual cottages. America has trailers, tents, log cabins and tar paper shacks; it has suburban colonials and stucco villas; it has seventeenth-century saltboxes and urban row houses. Any of the above could have a cottage garden. Of course, the very old and picturesque English cottages give their gardens an air of antiquity. There is little of this ancient aura around American gardens; American society is much too mobile.

A garden makes a
difference. Larry Wilson.
Memphis, Tennessee, May.

It is the homes of the very rich that pass from generation to generation; otherwise, it is rare for a man to raise his children in the same house in which he grew up. People simply move more frequently in America, for a variety of reasons. Often a couple won't start to garden until their children leave home and they move into a smaller house. While a few of the gardens shown here have been in existence for more than thirty years, the great majority are between five and ten years old, which is practically brand-new for a garden. It is also rare to buy a house that already has a garden of any sort, so most Americans start from scratch whenever they move. As a result, antiquity is not a hallmark of our cottage gardens; youthful exuberance and an air of experimentation are more characteristic.

In our vision of an ideal cottage garden, the plot is enclosed by a wall, fence or low hedge. This is almost always true in England; it is much less often the case in America. New England is the only part of this country where the gardens are usually enclosed; this is one reason why the yards of that region look most like our idea of a cottage garden. But in the rest of America, fenced gardens are in the minority. The effect overall is a much greater relationship between the gardens and the surrounding landscape than exists in English gardens on this scale. With the openness of American gardens comes their immediacy; there is no frame between you and the flowers. You are looking at the garden, you are in the garden.

Is a cottage garden a country garden? Not necessarily. Some large cities in America have abundant cottage gardens; look at San Francisco or Seattle. Many small gardens can be found at the edges of small or medium-size urban centers, in old neighborhoods of San Antonio or Memphis, for example. Even skyscraper cities like Chicago or Manhattan have a few islands of open ground set aside for allotments or community gardens, an urban form of cottage garden. Of course, there are country cottage gardens, too: the yards of farms, large or small, or little plots in rural villages. These could be in any part of this country; it is simply a matter of finding them.

Arthur Wallace
weeding the clematis.
Jonesboro, Arkansas, May.

So much for the outline of the garden. Now to the plants. Students of gardening have very specific ideas about what is appropriate to plant. But those ideas have no bearing at all on the American cottage garden. So-called classic English cottage flowers became classic because they were cheap, easily available, easy to grow and propagate; they were also useful, as a source of either food or medicine. The same criteria have determined many of America's favorite cottage flowers. Some are the same as the English classics, many are totally different. Because of America's many climates, the cottage flowers of one region don't correspond at all to those half a continent away. Herbs have always had a place in the cottage garden, and these accommodating plants are among the most universally grown species in both European and American gardens. A mixture of vegetables, herbs and flowers is very characteristic of the economy of cottage plots, both here and abroad. (Vegetables, in fact, are much more a part of the American cottage garden than may appear from our photographs; but tomatoes and corn look pretty much the same from Maryland to Montana, so we might be forgiven for concentrating on the flowers instead.)

The use of native plants is another time-honored tradition of cottage gardens, and here, obviously, the American garden resembles no other. In some cases wildflowers like Queen Anne's lace or the orange day lily are really European or Asian garden flowers that have made a place for themselves in the wild American landscape.

Many cottage gardeners are not aware that when they bring these plants back into the garden, they are simply bringing them full circle. Wildflowers have always been popular because they are pretty, they are free and they have proved that they can survive. In America this last consideration is infinitely more important than it is in England, because the climates here are so harsh, so diverse and, frankly, hard to figure out. There is a great deal of interest now in growing native plants, so more of them are available than ever before. Not that all American natives are easy to grow; many are incredibly reluctant to be tamed. In general, cottage gardeners are likely to choose the most readily available natives and not bother with fussy rarities.

Cottage gardeners usually start with easy and familiar plants. But because of the quixotic nature of cottage gardeners, I should also mention that difficult and bizarre plants have always had a home in the humble garden. In the early English gardens there was great interest in what were called "florist flowers." This term referred to hybrid forms, special double flowers or oddly colored sports, often developed and cultivated by the cottagers themselves. In the seventeenth century much of the interest in peculiar tulips arose, originally, from the cottage gardens; amateur enthusiasts also produced many of the exotic forms of primula and dianthus we know today. This kind of specialized cultivation can also be found in American cottage gardens. We tried to avoid the gardens of real specialists, since such gardens sometimes lose their easygoing charm and diverse appeal. But a garden of hundreds of iris, many hybridized by the gardener himself, can still be a cottage garden; likewise a yard filled with cactus, roses or giant dahlias.

I will go into greater detail about the flowers which characterize the American cottage garden in a separate chapter. For now, the most important thing to remember is that true cottage gardeners don't select their plants for what is "appropriate." They simply grow what they want to grow. If you see gardeners struggling to grow mignonette, more than likely they have read books about cottage gardens and are trying to create one. That is the point at which it is no longer a real American cottage garden.

*Giverny in
Salt Lake City,
Utah, August.*

Although there can be a wide range of plants grown in most parts of America, certain planting trends are apparent within each region. And in spite of the intense individuality of cottage gardens, elements of planning and design are remarkably consistent throughout a region. One of the most interesting aspects of the American cottage garden is how it reveals indigenous style. In some places a very subtle but consistent mood or outlook apparent in the gardens exists regardless of the originality of the individual gardener. In some areas the style develops from adaptations to the limits of climate or landscape particular to one part of the country. In others the historical development of a region plays a part. These indigenous styles contribute enormously to the atmosphere of each region of the country. I will examine them in detail in separate chapters.

Cottage gardens were the original organic gardens. This was dictated by economy more than by ideology. Expensive fertilizer and sprays were beyond the budget of most cottagers. Today in America some of that has changed. It is almost impossible to grow hybrid tea roses in most parts of America without spraying them, and most cottage gardeners will not give up their roses. In the vast agricultural regions of this country, chemical pest control is a fact of everyday life, and gardeners in those areas use what is available. But many cottage gardeners still do demonstrate that there are great numbers of plants that can be grown without chemical intervention. In gardens where edibles and ornamentals mix, most gardeners don't spray anything.

Organic fertilizer is still preferred; the majority of cottage gardeners have their compost piles hidden away somewhere. Animal manures are widely used in rural areas. Compost and manure are invaluable for soil improvement, a major concern of gardeners everywhere in this country.

It is a common misconception that because cottage gardens are small and appear nonchalant in their organization, they need little care. I should say, emphatically, that these are *not* low-maintenance gardens. It requires a lot of knowledgeable cultivation to grow many plants in a small space. While some crops are at their peak, others are being brought along to fill the space the minute the first bunch starts to wane. Every tendril of every vine is directed and secured. The soil is constantly being renewed to support all this abundant growth. Many cottage gardeners don't make use of laborsaving techniques available to the home gardener; most of these gardens are still watered by hand (some not even from a hose). Mulch is seldom seen. Indeed, many cottage gardeners don't *want* to save labor; the labor is what they love. These gardeners are not trying to get out of the work of the garden. They enjoy the process almost as much as the result.

Who makes cottage gardens in America? In England they were traditionally the gardens of the lower classes. In America today class is a fairly murky issue; it is better to say that gardens are influenced by the education, ethnic background and wealth of their creators. There is a close and unfortunate connection between money and gardening: The more money you have, the farther up you go into the middle class, the less likely it becomes that you will create a cottage garden. At some point education gets in the way, self-consciousness takes over and you find that you can no longer bear to have phlox and marigolds in the same bed and you simply must get the squash out from under the zinnias. A great many people, once they have the money, feel that they must pay someone else to make them a garden; you can never have a cottage garden by paying for it. Also, people with comfortable incomes usually buy houses and yards to match, and a large yard often works against a cottage garden; the plants are swamped by too much space.

So we seem to be saying that cottage gardens are made by people with little education, little money and little space. But the exceptions are so numerous that they almost seem to disprove all of that. One of the great anomalies is that more than a few doctors make cottage gardens. Many doctors like to garden, and some create extensive and elegant settings for their homes, but just as many choose a more humble mode of expression. (One of our doctor gardeners, in Natchez, has both kinds of garden.) You could hypothesize about this odd fact, but I have no real explanation; it is just an interesting discovery. Also among the professionals, teachers are quite commonly cottage gardeners. Architects never make this kind of garden; they are usually too absorbed in questions of design. Setting plays some part in determining who will garden and who won't: An accountant in a small town in a rural area might make a cottage garden; one in the suburbs almost never will. The suburbs in general are the most discouraging setting for a cottage garden. Gardeners will fight terrible soil, drought, frost or insects, but few can fight the stifling peer pressure of the suburbs.

Older people are more likely to make cottage gardens than younger people. Many retired people move to smaller houses and must live on smaller incomes; often, too, a compact garden is the only kind they can manage without help. But I think the main reason is that older gardeners, regardless of income or education, have long ago discarded any notion of making a garden to fit other people's ideas. Senior citizens garden for themselves, and they do so with wonderful boldness and originality. Often they have been gardening for decades and proceed with great assurance. Others begin when they retire; they are learning every day and their gardens are fresh and enthusiastic. This is not to say that there are no young cottage gardeners; you will meet several on these pages. Texas has a whole generation of energetic, youthful gardeners who are creating striking cottage plots. In Seattle it seems as if half the population, young or old, are cottage gardeners. By the way, if age may determine a cottage gardener to some extent, sex seems to play no part. I have no solid statistics at all, but our experience convinced us that men and women garden in equal numbers and on equal terms across America.

Ethnic background may contribute as well to the making of a cottage gardener. Gardening is much more a fact of life in other countries, and recent immigrants to America frequently bring with them the traditions of their homelands. We will examine these traditions in the regions where they are most apparent. After several generations this ethnic distinction becomes less pronounced, but continues to contribute to the flavor of certain regions.

Of all the factors that can contribute to the making of a cottage gardener, heredity is by far the most important. Virtually every gardener we met was inspired to garden by someone in his or her family. Father, mother, grandparent, great-aunt—somewhere back in the family there was a gardener. We all should feel the importance of this. It is possible for us to encourage the next generation of American gardeners. It is rare for someone with no gardening in the family to turn to it. And the children of gardeners are likely to make original and personal gardens because they are not merely absorbing design dictates from books.

This brings us to what I feel is the essential spirit of cottage gardening: unselfconsciousness. There are many ways of describing what we mean by a cottage garden, but we can never resolve a definition into more than a series of loose guidelines. As you will see from these pages, it would be hard to say how the gardens shown could possibly all be included in one definition. But what they all do have in common is their unselfconsciousness. These gardens are not trying to be anything, to show anything other than a single person's love of flowers. This love may be shown by a highly ordered, meticulous display; it may be evident in a wild and eccentric arrangement that corresponds to a very obscure notion of beauty. These gardens are not created for anyone else; the idea of an audience does not exist. All the gardeners we met were pleased that we stopped to admire their work, but the universal response to our admiration was surprise, as if it hadn't occurred to them that anyone was looking.

Rose cottage.
Seattle, Washington, July.

After unselfconsciousness, the most notable characteristic of cottage gardens is their generosity. The gardens make an effort to share their joy with everyone in sight. They are more often in the front yard than in the back. The flamboyant colors can be seen blocks away; the plants push out over the sidewalk to greet us. And these are not just gardens to look at. The vegetables are for picking and giving away. The flowers are there to be cut. Although the gardens are small, there is nothing precious about them; the gardener pushes through the beds, collecting an armload of flowers for the table, for a neighbor, for visitors like us, who received impromptu bouquets or enough vegetables for a week every time we stopped the car.

Some readers may thumb through these pages and think, "But these gardens are so *ordinary*." And they are, in the sense that they often have no special assets, nothing striking or astonishing about them. They are made by people all around us, and they could be made by anyone. That is one of the points of this book. It is lovely to fantasize about the magnificent English gardens that adorn many of the gardening books available. But come down out of the clouds. Stop dreaming and start making a garden of your own, as the gardeners in this book have done. Once you start to work, you may decide that the achievements shown here are not so slight as you imagined. I personally don't find these gardens ordinary at all; like all forms of folk art, they are created out of homely, familiar materials, but the results are deeply expressive and extraordinary.

Few gardens offer more pure and simple enjoyment than cottage gardens. You don't have to know anything about horticulture to understand them; garden history is equally irrelevant. But cottage gardens offer more than the exuberant joy the photographs convey. These gardens have a great deal to teach anyone who wants to garden in America. They prove that you don't need much money or much space. You don't need the "right" plants or the "right" tools. They remind us that gardeners learn to garden by gardening, by committing mistakes in the open air and by learning from them. They teach us that gardening goes on in even the most unlikely corners of the United States, and they offer us clues to deal with the most difficult climates. They show, over and over, that the featureless space of a cramped yard can be transformed by color and fragrance into a private and inviting wonderland. To anyone struggling over charts and color schemes, to those of us who lie awake hoping the new lilies are just the right shade of red, these gardens whisper, impertinently, "Relax. Enjoy." Cottage gardens help us to remember the things that matter, to keep in mind that beauty goes beyond taste and beyond style. They remind us all, in a thousand ways,
that the only reason to garden is for love.

The South ❧ *Louisiana* ❧ *Mississippi*

It can't be said that spring comes first to the Deep South—in California the hint of spring persists from December until February—but spring does come first to the South in the ways most of us recognize. Spring is the season at which the South excels, and southern gardens present the most unforgettable images of this stirring time: broad sweeps of narcissus under trees just beginning to bud; formal ranks of tulips marching up the walk to an eighteenth-century doorway; glowing pink and purple azaleas beneath ghostly curtains of Spanish moss. These are the images that represent for many the quintessential American garden. In fact, these gardens are unique, the result of conditions of climate and culture specific to this region. They are no more representative of American gardening than a cactus collection or a redwood forest. They do, however, have a richly romantic aura and a feeling of history that appeal to us all.

The most characteristic gardens of the Deep South are not cottage gardens as we have defined them or as we will see them in other parts of America; but it is interesting to look at the development of garden style in the Deep South to understand where the cottage garden fits in or why, in some areas, it barely exists at all.

Gardening in the Deep South has much stronger ties to history than in most parts of America. Early settlers in this region may not have been the scions of European aristocracy that they would have us believe, but as soon as these pioneers had prospered in America, they set about creating a setting for themselves that could be recognized as aristocratic in Old World terms. So the perfect eighteenth-century houses of Charleston or New Orleans were matched by painstakingly formal yards typical of that era. But as the Delta wealth was swelling and the magnificent plantations of the nineteenth century came into being, a new garden style was taking hold in England: the "naturalistic" landscape garden. Although the landscapes of Capability Brown et al. required as much manipulation of nature as a formal parterre, the result was a garden that looked like nature in its ideal state.

Southern comfort: camellias.
Natchez, Mississippi, March.

Bananas and tulips, also calendulas,
daffodils, crape myrtle, honeysuckle.
New Orleans, Louisiana, March.

This was a style perfectly suited to the plantations and for the rich and rolling countryside that makes up this region. Although the dominant plants of the new landscapes, the azaleas, were in fact Oriental species, there are native species of rhododendron from this area, and the foreign species looked right at home; they settled in and flourished as they seldom do in England. The formal garden is by its nature confined; the new style allowed the garden to stretch out into the wilderness for many acres. Formality was not forsaken—the grounds around the house often kept to the early mode; the new style simply broadened the range of display.

The small, formal, highly managed urban plot and the broad acres of plantation landscape had one important factor in common: the reliance upon a sizable labor force. These are not gardens made by or for one person. Even after the abolition of slavery a tradition of household servants persisted here longer than anywhere in the United States; today it is one of the few places where household help is still common in the homes of the middle class. With inexpensive and good labor available, few people do all their own gardening.
This works against the creation of cottage gardens.

Even though the great plantations have not existed in their original form for over a century, enough survives of those extraordinarily beautiful houses and landscapes to perpetuate their legend throughout the Delta; the plantation style still haunts southern gardens in a way that may be called the Reign of the Azalea. This plant seems to represent all the dreams of the Old South; homeowners fill their half-acre lots as if the azalea by its radiance could turn a suburban subdivision into Tara. There is no denying the virtues of this shrub—it has a long blooming season, makes a manageable evergreen shrub and thrives in the climate and soil of the region with almost no effort. But in most backyards the azalea is not a part of the garden; rather, it takes the place of gardening.

Pansies and cherry blossom.
Natchez, Mississippi, March.

A small yard full of azaleas requires no thought and little effort, and for one or two months of the year it almost looks like a garden. But a real cottage garden expresses much more interest in the plant world than could be satisfied by one fairly static plant; a cottage garden also requires much more effort and attention. I suppose I should be glad that yards are filled with azaleas rather than no flowers at all. But in cities like New Orleans, with lovely houses and cottage-size plots, it seems a shame that so many yards are crammed with just one not very interesting species. When you come upon a yard without an azalea, you feel at once that this is the home of a dedicated gardener.

Formality is not just a superficial style in the South; it shapes an entire way of life. Just as the heightened manners and social strictures of the plantation aristocracy struggled to keep the wilderness out of the drawing room, clipped box hedges, espalier fruit trees and carpet bedding signified that cultivation had triumphed over the rampant plant world on every side. Even today gardening here is based more on reduction than construction—cutting back rather than urging to grow. Frequent rain, high humidity and warm temperatures contribute to a terrifying rate of growth in many species, cultivated or not. A formal garden structure emphasizes the line drawn between desirable plants and weeds. But this seldom appeals to the avid gardener, whose enthusiasm tends to be inclusive rather than exclusive. Southern cottage gardeners frequently explore the accessories or techniques of the formal garden—topiary and espalier, for example—but a true formal garden is too severe a form of expression to satisfy them. The cottage gardens of this region do, nonetheless, convey a greater sense of control than we will see in other places, as well as a greater concern with form.

Local color:
kerria, azalea and oak.
Natchez, Mississippi, March.

Yes, in spite of all this history, there are cottage gardens in the Deep South. Somewhere between the plantation and the formal styles, between the azaleas and the clipped hedges of tea olive, are individuals who relentlessly make gardens for themselves, regardless of what is around them. Of course, in the rich southern spring, so much of the countryside is awash with flowers that it is hard to discern who is a cottage gardener and who isn't. The many varieties of flowering trees have a place in every kind of garden, grand or humble. Bulbs, too, are indispensable: crocus, narcissus and tulips in traditional gardens; the more out-of-the-way or outrageous genera *(Allium, Amaryllis, Frittilaria)* in cottage yards. Wisteria and the soft yellow sweeps of *Rosa banksiae* 'Lutea' wrap porches and climb trellises in gardens of rich and poor alike. Magnolias, gardenias and camellias contribute glossy foliage and unreal waxwork flowers to yards on every scale. And, of course, the azalea.

The fading of spring sorts out the cottage gardeners from those who just go along with the azaleas for the ride. Look for unusual iris species—*Iris spuria* or some of the appealing natives, *I. fulva* or *I. brevicaulis.* Watch for more surprising bulb species—crinum, haemanthus, tuberose, nerine. Instead of subsiding into green as the temperatures rise, the cottage garden begins to flare with color as summer begins—deep blue, lavender or pink larkspur; sunny coreopsis; flamelike ipomopsis, a vivid local weed. Hybrid tea roses are often displayed in the stilted elegance of a formal rose bed, but they have a very different look in the cottage garden, where they are likely to be surrounded by a rainbow assortment of other flowers. Semitropical species add to the confusion along the Gulf. In one New Orleans yard, shrimp plant and alstroemeria were the predominant flowers, with mustard greens on the side; in another, bridal wreath, a familiar hardy shrub in the North, bloomed next to a tropical cycad.

Cottage window.

Natchez, Mississippi, March.

The semitropical mix gets much more noticeable as you move down into Florida. This state is a region all its own, since there is a wealth of plant material that will grow here and nowhere else. Florida is also beyond the sweep of history that formed the gardens of the Delta, so cottage gardens here have a much more impromptu air. With so many retired people and so many recently arrived Hispanics, cottage gardens in Florida are abundant, original and much more diverse than the gardens of neighboring states.

Many of the most engaging gardens in the Deep South are created by the people who have always done the gardening—African-Americans. In New Orleans, with flowers as with food, the most inventive and personal approach is found in tiny, cluttered yards off the tourist track. In these yards few garden conventions exist. The gardeners grow what they want to eat and they grow what they want to see. These yards are not without their occasional azaleas, but there is a great deal more besides.

Out in the countryside of the Deep South it is the small-scale farms up away from the broad Delta plantations that tend to produce gardens of interest, if you can find them. In rural villages of the region it is usually the older gardeners, black or white, who are least concerned with tradition and who grow the most surprising variety of plants. Some of the old Delta towns, like Natchez, demonstrate an interesting mingling of garden styles. The yards—and the extraordinary houses—are frequently too large to encourage an intensely planted plot, but they are too small for the expansive plantation style. Many of them feature exquisite formal plantings.

Double peach.
New Orleans, Louisiana,
March.

Others are a nice blending of the plantation with the cottage style—graceful and flowery landscapes of loose structure that respond to the remarkable landforms of the area. There were water-filled bayous here several centuries ago, but the water table has dropped, leaving picturesque small-scale terraces or gentle ravines through backyards all over town. These are enhanced with plantings, paths and seats to make delightful garden glades. Are they cottage gardens? Not by the usual definitions, but they are personal and have immediate appeal.

Even the most passionate cottage gardeners of the Deep South tend to lose their enthusiasm for the out-of-doors when the long, hot summer begins in earnest. This is when the true beauty of the formal garden can be appreciated; abstract shapes of green seem wonderfully restful in July. Cottage gardens in the South rely more on trees and shrubs for midsummer structure than do northern gardens, partly because perennials and biennials are finished blooming so early, in part because in July and August all that most southern gardeners want from their yards is a cool place in the shade to sit down. Many gardens here are created as a background for sitting outdoors; they have an inviting, relaxing air of leisure at midsummer that more energetic northern yards lack. With the short growing season in the North, it sometimes seems as if the gardeners are too busy to sit and enjoy their efforts; it is more usual to walk through those gardens than to sit in them. But the South has a slower rhythm, and the pleasures of the summer are often best sampled in a hammock. Perhaps this is why southern plantings offer so many delights other than those merely visual; fragrance is an inescapable aspect of these gardens' appeal. As you rock in your hammock, the heavy scent of honeysuckle or tuberose wafts by. You can stop weighing heavy questions of garden style and enjoy.

Dr. William F. Calhoun;
Elgin. Natchez,
Mississippi, March.

Natchez is a living museum of antebellum splendor. The houses are
magnificent, and many still retain their original furnishings. Elgin is
by any reckoning one of the most outstanding of these mansions,
and it also has the attraction of two very different kinds of garden.

Most of the great plantation grounds of Elgin have been divided and
sold, but the remaining twenty-five acres around the house are sufficient to screen it from most signs of the late twentieth century and to
preserve elements of the classic plantation landscape. The carriage
drive circles under heavy festoons of Spanish moss hanging from the
live oaks and magnolias, planted in 1843. The imposing Greek
Revival portico from the same period faces out across a lawn toward
massive azaleas. But the first house at Elgin was built shortly after
1792, when the land was deeded to the original settler. The early
building still survives and joins the Greek portico at the back at a
right angle, and this part of the estate's history has its garden, too. In
front of the original house is a delightful cottage plot, perfectly in
keeping with the scale and style of the earlier building.

Dr. William F. Calhoun, the present owner of Elgin, is an enthusiastic gardener. Before the Calhouns bought Elgin, in 1976, the
estate was owned by two impoverished gentlewomen who struggled to
keep the place through the Depression. They had no money, but
they would not give up their garden. Dr. Calhoun relates how they
grew only flowers that would come back and multiply year after year,
plants that could survive without expensive fertilizers or pest con-
trols. These tough survivors still contribute to Dr. Calhoun's garden:
Thick masses of tiny but heavily fragrant narcissus line the paths and
start blooming almost in midwinter. A rare white lycoris with a pink
blush thrives in his garden but refuses to be transplanted elsewhere.
To these and others Dr. Calhoun has added his own favorites,
among them hybrid tea roses. I wondered how Dr. Calhoun, a pedia-
trician, managed to come home every day for lunch and for a bit of
time in his garden. "Well," he said with a smile, summing up the
speed of life in the Deep South, "there's not a lot of traffic in
Natchez."

The South ❧ Tennessee ❧ Kentucky ❧ Arkansas

The Middle South is a dramatic contrast to the broad Delta states we have just seen. Even though there are rich, flat farming lands along the Mississippi River, Tennessee, Arkansas and Kentucky were never a part of the true plantation tradition. There are areas well suited for farming here—the whole region is overwhelmingly agricultural—but they are broken up by the waves of hills and mountain ranges that crisscross this region. These fragments of farmland, in the past and today, are productive enough to provide modest existences for the independent families that struggle to hold on to them, but the geography of the region has always fought the consolidation necessary for more ample profit. Both in the past and today the geography and economy have worked against an outside labor force, whether slave or paid. The people here work hard for themselves, and one thing they do for themselves when they are not working is make gardens.

This region has a landscape of almost universal appeal. The mountains are inspiring but not as overpowering as the younger, fiercer ranges of the West, and they are clothed with forests of amazing diversity. It is only the serious naturalist who can identify the bewildering variety of trees that occur when the eastern hardwood forest meets the southern coastal woodland. The climate that fosters this landscape is no less attractive: There is much precipitation but lower humidity than on the coast or farther south; warm temperatures but more moderate than in the lowlands; hot summers but long and temperate springs and falls.

Memphis is the urban hub of this ring of states, a green and leisurely metropolis sprawling along the Mississippi. The properties within the city vary greatly in size, and garden styles complement this diversity. The large houses with spacious yards around them resemble their counterparts farther south with the presence of rhododendrons and a tendency toward a formal landscape design; these are usually gardens managed with outside help.

Old roses. Edythe Browne.
Raleigh, Tennessee, May.

The ornamental and
the edible: broccoli
and bachelor buttons, lettuce
and larkspur. Larry Wilson.
Memphis, Tennessee, May.

The smaller yards are the ones likely to be bursting with flowers. There are also properties of moderate size (over half an acre) with loose, naturalistic plantings of flowers. Shade is a major factor in gardening here. Because of the great summer heat in this low-lying city, no one with old trees is eager to give them up; but shade limits the range of flowers, although many of the standard perennials grown with full sun in the North benefit from partial shielding from the southern sun. The shade quandary has encouraged a great deal of interest in the woodland plants of the region, which are abundant and beautiful. A shady woodland garden is more subtle and less overtly flowery than the compact and sunny spaces we think of as belonging to the cottage genre. (One gardener from Montana returned from a visit to North Carolina and was asked what he thought of the gardens of that state. ''Gardens?'' he exclaimed. ''There ain't nothing in them but trees!'') But these shade gardens are often just as personal and unselfconscious as our cottage type and should be acknowledged. Some of the most widely used and interesting natives for shade are varieties of penstemon, green dragon and the quite spectacular Indian paint *Spigelia marilandica*. The oak-leaf hydrangea is a lovely native shrub.

The overall interest in gardening is immediately noticeable here; there is quite a lot of garden visiting (which is relatively rare in other parts of the United States but is an enjoyable form of social and horticultural exchange in England and France) and a lot of garden talk. One woman who moved to Memphis from the North recalled her first southern garden party: ''I couldn't believe it. Here were all these well-dressed, cultured women, standing around and talking about compost!'' These are not all necessarily cottage gardeners, but there is a general sense here that gardening is a worthwhile way to spend time, offering more than a required green setting for a home. This is the kind of ''gardening atmosphere'' which encourages gardens on every level.

The end of the road.
Peggy Bingham.
Ashland, Mississippi, May.

In general throughout the South the interest in gardening stops short
of botany or nomenclature; gardeners here have little interest in the
specifics of a plant. They learn how to grow it and how to place it in
a garden; they have little curiosity about its name or its relationship
to the rest of the plant world. There are always outstanding exceptions to this—most rose growers can recite the pedigrees of any of
their huge number of varieties, and there are some real students of
horticulture here and there. For the most part southern gardeners
were good-humored and unembarrassed about not knowing what the
plants were in their gardens; they were amused when I knew the
name of something, as if I had performed a magic trick. And of
course, it makes little difference in their gardens. In the Middle
South, in general, there is a wide mixture of well-known and unusual
species and increasing sophistication in the use of perennials and
bulbs, both traditional and native. Who cares if they call spigelia
"worm grass"? I can say it in Latin, but they can grow it, and that,
in the cottage garden, is always the bottom line.

The South is the Kingdom of the Rose, the hybrid tea above all.
Most hybrid varieties produce four flushes of bloom through a long
season in the South, May through November, with peaks in mid-
May and September. This is scarcely a carefree plant, but the continuous production of flowers is worth the effort of feeding and endless
spraying. There are very few southern gardens without some roses
and quite a lot with many. In one Memphis backyard of less than a
quarter acre, 270 named varieties made a stunning show of color.
Some of the meticulous raised beds were neatly edged with iris or
sweet william for early bloom; in others tuberoses were set out after
frost to provide cut flowers and fragrance through the summer. Out
in Raleigh, a suburb of Memphis, Edythe Browne has made a spe-
cialty of the old rose varieties. These, unlike the hybrid teas, make
magnificent shrubs, bold statements of form and color. They don't
really lend themselves to organization; Mrs. Browne has wisely let
them find their own way in her spacious, half-wild landscape. A pale
gold climber twined with white clematis up an oak; "Prairie Prin-
cess" and the old red moss looped over one another as Queen
Anne's lace popped up from beneath.

Madonna lilies.
Bardwell, Kentucky, May.

This is not a very old garden—about ten years—but its wildness and the antiquity of the rose species give it a feeling of timelessness. You feel as if you were caught in the thorn thicket around Sleeping Beauty's castle.

Besides the subtle shady gardens and the rosaries, the middle South has more than its share of classic colorful and exuberant cottage gardens. Here we begin to see one of the most noticeable characteristics of American cottage gardens: Although confined within a small space, the flowers spill out and take over any additional space they can colonize. The driveway, the median strip along the curb, even the cracks of the sidewalk are not safe once such a garden takes off. Larry Wilson's plot in Memphis (seen on page 16) is a fine example. Mr. Wilson is a botanist with a special interest in native plants, so his front yard is crammed with bright native coreopsis, oenothera and phlox; his, shrublike *Baptisia lactea* provides blue-green foliage and fat pods that turn almost black in the fall. Behind his small house is a perfect cottage yard, where dianthus and lettuce line the walk and broccoli blooms with bachelor buttons.

The surrounding states—Arkansas, Kentucky and the northern, hilly parts of Mississippi—are equally rich in small, personal gardens. Arkansas has one of the highest populations of retired people in the country, and wherever there are retired people with yards, more than likely there are cottage gardens. But there are young enthusiasts as well, like Arthur Wallace of Jonesboro, Arkansas, who started off mowing lawns for people and discovered he has an unexpected flair with flowers. "One of my clients started giving me pieces of her flowers, and I worked at making them spread." His own garden has been in the making only four years, but it is already straining the confines of a yard shared with three young children and a very active puppy. "We have to expand the house, but to do that I have to move my grapes," which he expects to bear fruit for the first time this year. "I'm holding off construction till after the harvest. I'm not sure how they will take the move, and I'd sure like to taste some grapes before I have to start over."

Mr. and Mrs. M. S. Cook;
roses and sweet william.
Dublin, Kentucky, May.

We were standing in their driveway when the Cooks arrived home from church. (Geneva Cook got out of the truck holding the massive family Bible and continued to hold it throughout our visit.) They were somewhat surprised but utterly cordial when we explained that we had stopped when we saw their "scarecrow"—an arresting, if gruesome, gibbet of two dead starlings fluttering above the vegetables. Mr. Cook said he didn't think it helped much, but it made him feel better to look at it.

The Cooks had been farmers out on a larger property but had retired and moved to this house in Dublin, Kentucky, seven years ago. A lot of effort has gone into improving the red clay soil typical of the region, but the flourishing stand of vibrant orange lilies and climbing roses showed that the effort was worthwhile.

Besides gardening, the other leisure activity of this close couple (the Cooks have been married fifty years) is fishing in the tiny pond they dug behind the house. "I never held much with fishing," said

Geneva Cook. "It was always my husband carrying on about it. But one evening there I caught myself a ten-pound catfish. Well, I was so excited, when I went to church the next day I just stood up and testified to everyone and the Lord about that fish."

We passed up, with much regret, a catfish supper, but the Cooks told us they'd have some ready the next time we stopped by.

Peggy Bingham and her eighty-year-old mother arrived at 6:00 A.M. to drive us seventy miles down to Mississippi to see Janie Porter's garden. Miss Bingham's aunt, Inez McGaughy, lives in Ashland, Mississippi, with her husband, Fred, who runs the general store. Inez is a gardener. The gerberas she had raised from seed were just starting to bloom, along with pansies and sweet william. Inez and Fred often drive around the countryside after church on Sundays, looking at the crops and visiting the gardens of friends.

Janie Porter's garden is as far from anything as one could imagine. Ashland itself, with a population of 531, is already pretty far off the

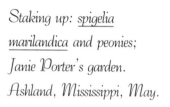

Staking up: spigelia
marilandica and peonies;
Janie Porter's garden.
Ashland, Mississippi, May.

track, but to get to Mrs. Porter's, we drove for miles on unmarked
dirt roads through untouched scrub oak and pine. There is probably
not another house for ten miles. Mrs. Porter keeps two terrifying
dogs, but the isolation of her home doesn't bother her. "I don't have
no worry here."

Janie Porter is seventy-five years old and has been gardening here
since 1957. She was reluctant to have us take her portrait which was
regrettable, since she is a remarkable-looking woman, her face
smooth, round, black, and highlighted by a flashing gold front tooth;
with her slim legs and short skirt, she looked less than fifty. "I had a
heart attack in '72, but I'm fine since then. Doctor says gardening
keeps me going."

It is a garden that would exhaust a far younger worker. Mrs. Porter's
garden is a loose expanse of yard on both sides of her house, more or
less enclosed by a variety of wire fences. Shrubs, small trees, rose
bushes and shrublike perennials make up the larger masses but can
scarcely be said to provide structure; overall organization is not a

major concern. Each plant dwells on its own patch of immaculate bare earth. (When I suggested that some form of mulch might cut down on her weeding time, Mrs. Porter was intrigued; she had never heard of mulch.) There was not a weed anywhere, and even though the black walnut trees shading the front of the property were dropping masses of catkins, the ground beneath was swept clean. There were some real surprises among the traditional cottage plants: a huge mound of *Penstemon pinifolius*; a spectacular yellow tree peony (pronounced pe-ó-ny here); brilliant *Gladiolus byzantinus*. Janie has a typically southern indifference to plant names. "I just buy what looks good in that catalog. Then, can you believe, they send me things for free." She orders mostly from "Burp's." "And you know, most things do grow."

With the characteristic generosity of cottage gardeners, Janie Porter was eager to share her plants. We all admired her tall, deep red weigela. "What?" she asked Peggy Bingham. "You don't have one of those? Well, you just go get you a piece of that."

The West Coast ❦ California

The West Coast offers two radically different views of paradise. Southern California is a radiant world of brilliant sunshine, blue water, deep suntans and brown chaparral. The Pacific Northwest is a lush and cool universe of endless evergreens, unlimited rainfall, overcast skies and snowcapped mountains. What they have in common is an extraordinary interest in gardens. The West Coast is truly gardening's Gold Coast.

Horticulture on every level has long been the mainstay of life in California. Patio gardeners tending their redwood tubs and giants of commercial agriculture have in common the inspiration of an amazing climate. Almost everyone who comes to California feels the urge to be out of doors most of the time—here is an entire culture devoted to outdoor activity of every kind. But while the swimming pool and the tennis court can still be reasonable attractions after retirement age, the surfboard and the dirt bike tend to lose their appeal early on. Gardening often fills the gap after the last wave.

A first-time visitor to Los Angeles can be overwhelmed by the broad range of unrecognizable and astonishing plants. At any time of the year there is stunning color from trees, vines and ground covers that originate from every part of the world. Because of this brilliant surface, it takes awhile to realize that this is not so much gardening as a kind of floral decor. People are expected to have gardens here, and so they do, in a variety of styles as ornate and artificial as the stage set houses they accompany: mission-style gardens; Chinese gardens; formal rose gardens; even southern plantation gardens. Like stage sets, these ''gardens'' are created and maintained by squads of experts. It is ironic that in this city apparently so full of gardens, you can scarcely find a homeowner with dirt on his hands. I don't want to disparage the trend in California that makes a lush and beautiful landscape a signature of the good life. It does result in some very pretty scenery. It just doesn't result in intimate or interesting cottage gardens.

Cottage garden devours house.
Laguna Beach, California, February.

Iris and bromeliads.
Charles Hill. Los Angeles,
California, February.

Style is a major concern in urban Southern California, and it has an unfortunately disconcerting effect on gardeners just starting out. The long years it can take to make a real garden seem inconceivable here; all those seasons of trying and failing while you discover what it is you want to grow are not allowed for. In Los Angeles a garden is something you have, not something you do; if the plantings aren't in perfect bloom, call someone up to bring in a border. And the tempting fact is there are so many professionals who can do just that, and do it beautifully. The eager amateur feels there is almost no way to participate except by paying the bill.

Because of this inhibiting concern with style, the cottage gardens of Southern California are an invaluable inspiration when you do find them. They exist as reminders of the essential wonder of the California climate: Anyone can garden here and have a great time. Forget the slick glamour of the celebrity magazines; that is not where you will discover gardens with a unique and unselfconscious point of view. It is scarcely surprising that the most interesting gardens in this city are made by those least concerned with style: the poor, the elderly, the Hispanics, the artists and the out-of-touch.

In the midst of Los Angeles the Spanish barrios burst with lively color; the gardens here display an unconventional order that defies clichés. Latin culture, which contributes so much to the look and feel of Southern California, is a major influence on the gardens of the inner city. Skilled Mexican and Central American gardeners are responsible for a great deal of the landscaping all over California; gardening would not be such an indispensable part of the good life on the West Coast if these excellent workers were not available. The gardens they make for themselves are frequently more inspired than the ones they work on to survive.

California classics.
Charles Hill. Los Angeles,
California, February.

Outside the ever-spreading environs of Los Angeles it is much easier to find cottagers. Throughout California high property values and high water rates combine to limit the size but not the ambitions of many gardens; this encourages the tendency to use every inch. Artificial watering is universal and essential for any form of gardening here, but cottage gardens make especially good use of water. Most have little or no space given over to grass, which requires the most frequent watering. Container growing is widespread, for several reasons: Plants can be grown in otherwise unusable space, on steps, porches or patios; although evaporation through the pot necessitates fairly frequent watering, plants are watered efficiently because no excess ground is watered. (Hidden drip systems can be tucked discreetly into the planters to make watering easier.) Containers can also provide special soil for plants with specific requirements; in alkaline areas of the West, for example, azaleas are grown in acid soil in pots. In spectacular mountain or rocky coastal sites, containers may be the only available spot of soil. Often these lavishly planted pots are like cottage gardens in miniature, with a mixture of material for extended bloom in several seasons.

The seasons run into one another in California but are generally divided into winter, which is cool and has some rain, if not a lot, and summer, which is hot and has no rain. Cool-weather annuals and so-called spring bulbs can be found flowering from October through May; semitropical material, hot-climate annuals and native plants stretch from spring through late fall. Traditional garden perennials are often not successful here; if they do survive, they are short-lived, more like biennials. Native and semitropical shrubs and vines are important for their prolonged bloom through the long, unrelieved hot spells.

Los Angeles luxuriance.
Bob Grimes. Los Angeles,
California, February.

Because of the vast range of plant material, gardens in California can develop in any number of unconventional ways. Cactus and succulents are a natural interest in this climate because of their drought tolerance; increasing water restrictions are winning these unusual plants more enthusiasts every summer. Many specimens of this group are so bizarre that no matter how often you see them used, they never look like a garden cliché. Even where water is available, spectacular agaves, aloes and yuccas can be used in the outermost areas of the garden, frequently as an ornamental but fairly threatening hedge.

Many California cottage gardeners follow very specific interests. Artist Charles Hill in Venice collects bromeliads and species of bamboo, which he utilizes in his paintings. At the other extreme are gardeners like Bob Grimes, who has one or two examples of thousands of species. He seems intent on discovering every known plant that will flourish in Los Angeles; the result is a wild botanical sampler, immaculately maintained, flowing up and down the steep canyon slopes around his mock–Queen Anne cottage.

Native plants have become more prevalent in landscape use in the past few years in California. Many municipal water departments offer incentives (or use threats) to encourage new customers to turn at least part of their property over to drought-tolerant species. This doesn't have much effect on most cottage gardeners, however, since their compact plots usually require much less water than the daily allotment, and most gardeners would gladly give up a daily shower in order to plant what they like.

Spring seedlings.
Bob Grimes. Los Angeles,
California, February.

Some natives do show up regularly in these gardens: Eschscholtzia, the gay and ubiquitous California poppy, pops up as casually as a weed and is often given space until it is time to plant something else. We saw it used as an early ground cover under rose bushes; the color confrontation when the roses bloomed later in the season was something I'm sorry we missed. Beautiful penstemons, either natives or hybrids, are available and are gaining in popularity. Some of the numerous attractive mimulus species are planted quite often. The spectacular Matilija poppy, *Romneya coulteri,* has made the move into gardens both here and up the coast as far as British Columbia. Over six feet tall, with lovely bluish gray foliage and a show-stopping bloom of dazzling white with a golden tuft of stamens, this is a native not to be missed.

Many warm-climate bulbs thrive and provide bloom in several seasons. This is the best climate in America for growing ranunculus, and everyone takes advantage of the fact; starting in midwinter, the rich colors of these fat, ruffled flowers glow in gardens of every kind. Freesia and paper-white narcissus start even earlier, often before Christmas. Most tulips are not successful, although people persist in trying. Crocosmia make enormous clumps of fiery color. Agapanthus, alstroemeria and calla lilies are so rampant they are considered fairly weedy ground covers.

Vines and shrubs are important to the gardens of California, both as structural elements and for the continuous bloom they can provide. Semitropical vines such as golden cup (solandra), stephanotis, plumbago and solanum aren't overpowering when they are in flower, but they continue blooming for months. Bougainvillea, of course, *is* overpowering and seems to bloom forever. Several species of jasmine perfume the winter months. Old-fashioned climbing and trailing roses are the most widely used varieties of America's favorite plant; hybrid tea roses are grown in California but don't have the enormous prevalence they do in other parts of the country. The climbers and shrub roses, however, are spectacular, starting in February with the warm-climate favorite *Rosa banksiae* 'Lutea.'

Ice plant and plum.
Ojai, California, February.

Because many of the best-known perennials are not successful or widely used in California, shrubs give necessary mass and substance to small gardens. Australia has contributed a few of the most commonly seen: Geraldton waxflower; bottlebrush; the innumerable species of eucalyptus. Some shrubby natives of interest are salvias, manzanitas and ceonothus, carpenteria and fremontia, encelia, galvesia (island snapdragon) and lavatera, the tree mallow.

There is a distinctive look to California gardens that goes beyond the wealth of exotic plant material, although the plants certainly contribute a great deal. California gardens have the feeling of being always new. In part, the short life-span of many of the plants is responsible. Annuals perform for a brief season and are then discarded; perennials often disappear after a year or so. Gardening in four seasons in a small space requires relentless replanting. Shrubs and vines often grow so vigorously that it is easier to take them out after a few years than to cut them back all the time. There is also a restless spirit of experimentation that gardeners catch when exposed to the California climate. There is simply so much to grow, how can anyone confine his ambitions to just a few species? Style affects this ever-changing look in the more upscale gardens. One year everyone is tired of ground covers and puts in paving; a sudden rage for Gertrude Jekyll will swell the borders with lavender and campanula. The real cottage gardeners tend to be unaware of that kind of shifting trend, but the lure of a new plant is harder to resist. Many of the most appealing gardens in California are those which convey the excitement of a gardener in this brave new world of things to grow. For those cottage gardeners, it is the content, not the style, that matters.

*Beatrice Wyatt's rock
garden; rocks and magnolia.
Ventura, California, February.*

At the end of a dead-end street under the freeway in Ventura, a kalei-
doscope of color tumbles into the road. You can see it from blocks
away. Most cottage gardens have a tendency to push beyond their
boundaries; this one, unimpeded by sidewalk or curb, almost stops
traffic. It is hard to believe that this astonishing spectacle is the
handiwork of one rather frail-looking woman in her eighties, but
even as we stopped to chat, Beatrice Wyatt worked without pause,
hauling dull, unpainted rocks over to a spot in the sun where she
could paint them (''I do like to be warm when I'm working''), then
taking back the dry, painted gems to be placed carefully in her
scheme. Mrs. Wyatt's only explanation for this incredible effort
is succinct: ''I like to keep busy.''

There are plants in this Watts Tower of a garden—huge twin aeoniums burst like headlights from an improvised planter of pottery shards and broken mirror—but even fiery kalanchoes seem a bit cowed by their setting. Overhead a magnificent magnolia is in full fragrant bloom. "Look at that thing," Beatrice Wyatt demands, laughing, in mock outrage. "I told them at the nursery I wanted a bush. And look what they gave me!" She darts away to pick up a blushing petal before it turns brown among her rocks. "Yes, I like to keep busy," she says again. "I like to eat. I like to sleep. And I like to go to church." Amen.

The West Coast ❧ The Pacific Northwest

A trip up the Pacific Coast from Southern California to Washington State features breathtaking scenery and a gradual and fascinating change in climate. The mist-shrouded rocky coast with its heavy blanket of vegetation breaks abruptly into blazing sun and hot brown hillsides as soon as the road turns inland. As you head north, slowly there are more and more trees; slowly there is less and less sun. There is abundant gardening along the way responding to the shifts in weather: The semitropical material drops out; succulents are less evident; shade becomes a greater part of the landscape. In San Francisco gardeners create vertical pictures with plants suited to cool and foggy weather that is also surprisingly dry. This city, with its lovely old houses and tiny plots, has always been rich in cottage gardens, and there is less of the stylish self-consciousness we found in Los Angeles. But it is in Washington that the contrast with Southern California is most dramatic. Just about the only plants that won't grow in Seattle are the plants that do best in L.A.—tropical sun lovers that resent moisture. In Seattle gardeners can expect thirty to forty inches of rain a year (other locations in the same county could get eighty); in Los Angeles twelve or fourteen inches are normal. Forty inches of rain are not excessive (compared with the hundred inches that could fall on Cedar Lake, Washington, in a year), but the generally cool weather and overcast skies make it more than sufficient for a garden.

Coastal Washington offers gardeners a climate without extremes, unless you count the extreme number of cloudy days. Winters provide enough cold for dormancy but not for prolonged periods of freezing. The summers can be warm and dry (relative to winter) but are seldom hot and are usually dry for only a month or two. In winter the gray and rainy weather is made to seem even more depressing by the short periods of daylight, while in summer the long, long days have a marked and favorable effect on flowers and gardeners alike.

Farm garden. Conway,
Washington, July.

Foxgloves. Conway,
Washington, July.

The climate of the Pacific Northwest is often compared with that of England; while there are marked differences, it is the closest to England we can get in America. One noticeable similarity is the sense you have from looking at the plants that nothing ever goes out of bloom. The seasons seem to overlap in impossible ways: In early July, sweet william was blooming as if it were May, but carrots in the same garden were ready to harvest. Basket-of-gold *(Aurinia saxatilis)*, one of the brightest spots of April, was in flower with dahlias. Foxgloves seem to bloom year-round. Changes in elevation add further confusion. A trip up to one of the mountain regions can rapidly roll back the seasons into winter. A few hundred feet can change late lilies and phlox to early spring anemones and erythronium. Those of us in the rest of America are accustomed to hearing with skepticism from English books that plants have a blooming period of two or three months; in the Pacific Northwest all that is true. The result is a greater density and lushness to the gardens; the bare spots and gaps that plague the rest of us just don't seem to happen here.

It is hardly surprising that this region has a long-standing and ever-widening interest in gardening. Even in the cosmopolitan centers, home and family life are principal preoccupations, and gardening fits well with those. The only real competition for people's time is from boating or mountain climbing, for which the region is also superbly suited.

From the beginning of the century until twenty or thirty years ago, well-trained garden help was available from floods of Asian immigrants; this labor force contributed to the highly manicured and expansive estate gardens of the wealthy. But the economy of this region does not encourage the widespread use of such labor anymore, and these days the Asian immigrants are more likely to be holding down well-paying white-collar jobs. Most of the property in the urban areas consists of small plots, kept by one or two people, and perfectly suited to cottage-style gardens.

Trailer park.
Near Mt. Rainier,
Washington, July.

Sophistication is very evident in the gardening around Seattle, but it is more likely to take the form of unusual, select plant material than self-conscious or imitative garden style. Because all the plants are temperate-zone species, they don't appear as exotic as the semitropical plants used farther south; it is only when you try to identify something that you realize it is a high-mountain flower from southern Chile or Japan. Some species look unfamiliar to easterners simply because they are growing so well. Heaths and heathers which barely cling to life in the Northeast make a lush and unrecognizable ground cover here.

Seattle is built primarily on a glacial moraine, which accounts for the abrupt ups and downs of the city and the characteristic arrangement of many of the houses, perched atop piles of rocks. The appealing small buildings—often in a distinctive, slightly Art Deco style—are more like real cottages than can be found in any other major city. There is usually a little soil immediately around the house; the ever present rocks are used to shore up the property above the sidewalk. This arrangement of rocks (often very elaborate) is an obvious site for rock plants, and the rock gardeners here are the most numerous and active in the United States. But you scarcely need to be an alpine expert to achieve a hanging garden of campanula and mountain phlox, centranthus and sedum. Species like these cascade down Seattle streets as casually as dandelions.

The moraine areas of the Pacific Northwest don't have much to offer in the way of soil. What dirt there is is usually thin and gravelly, and a great deal of effort goes into its improvement. Composting is *de rigueur* in this extremely environment-conscious region, but some gardeners go to greater extremes: Next to the front door of one tiny property was a large pile of decomposing manure (this in central Seattle). The arrangement of yards built up on walls does help with drainage during the soggy winter months.

Heather and rose.

Seattle, Washington, July.

All the classic border perennials are well represented in the gardens of the Pacific Northwest, usually looking larger than even a garden-catalog photo (as you proceed up to British Columbia, they get even bigger). The long days and long growing season combine for this lavish growth. There are surprisingly few trees in Seattle gardens—with the often overcast skies, no one seems eager for shade—but in much of the Pacific Northwest, shade is a significant part of the gardening landscape. The combination of shade and acid soil fosters the overwhelming popularity of one enormous genus, *Rhododendron*. The largest rhododendron collection in the world is established in this region, and there are innumerable specialized nurseries selling every obscure and outlandish variety. Although plenty of suburban yards feature the rhododendron as the familiar ribbon of color around a bleak foundation, there are also very sophisticated gardens by collectors. The interest in these plants is quite different here from in the South, where we saw them as the prevailing landscape feature. In the Deep South, in the large gardens where they are most successful, they are used in a more painterly fashion; the interest is in the masses of color in the landscape, rather than in unusual species or varieties. In the hot weather of the South, the small-leaf, tender Oriental azalea species are most widely grown; the broad-leaf, clustered-flower rhododendrons do better in a cool climate. (They all are botanically rhododendrons, but these are the ones we usually call by that name.) Through spring and early summer in the Pacific Northwest, these shrubs certainly cover a lot of ground, but by midsummer, when they have finished, it is clear that the rhododendrons are much less dominant than they are in the South.

Bather.
Seattle, Washington, July.

There is such diverse gardening here that when the rhododendrons are finished, they are scarcely missed. I, for one, was just as glad we were seeing this region in July.

The ever-popular rose is not absent from the garden scene here, although rose growers have to battle fungus and diseases which thrive in the humid weather. Like everything else, the roses are enormous. In one of my favorite Seattle gardens hybrid tea bushes were taller than the tiny house; it was hard to imagine how the gardener got in or out of his home.

It is impossible to declare which region of America has the ''best'' cottage gardens (I can't even decide which ones are my own favorites), but if you want to see the most small gardens in a small area, a trip to Seattle is a revelation. And when you see beyond the huge number of different and interesting plants and the obvious advantages of the weather, you realize that the delight of these gardens lies not in the spectacular flowers and how they are grown. The wonderful thing about gardening in Seattle is that so many people are doing it and sharing it with one another. This is what makes up a true ''climate'' for gardening, and it could be imitated in every part of our country, to the greater enjoyment of us all.

Paul Meadors with a rose for Pat;
sweet william and shasta daisies.
Coupeville, Washington, July.

Paul Meadors has lived outside Coupeville on Whidbey Island for almost fifty years. From an Army family—he was born at Fort Lewis in Washington—he and three brothers all served in the armed forces. With one brother he farmed these sixty acres and raised Black Angus; now the cattle are gone, and he mostly farms his garden. "I'm just an old bachelor. I start all my own seeds. End up giving most of it away." Paul Meadors proved that by filling the trunk of our car with carrots and beets. The mild island climate seldom has temperatures below ten degrees; last winter there was no frost at all. "The soil here's kind of gravelly." He has brought in loads of topsoil and makes liberal use of fertilizer and farm manure, evident in

the exceptional size of the flowers—a "Tropicana" rose was as big as a cabbage; petunias were the size of Paul Meadors's generous hand. I was amazed at the doronicum, which is often a negligible plant; here the doronicums resembled gerbera, with long stems and broad, glistening flowers. "My mother planted those," said Paul, "must be forty years ago. I keep them going." He admits to having had a stormy life in the past, but gardening has always been a comfort and a relaxation. He has been nursing a monkey puzzle tree *(Araucaria araucana)* since it was a few inches high; it is now about his height, slightly over six feet. "It hasn't done much for the past twenty years, but I think it's about ready to take off."

The Midwest

Travel is the best reminder of how distinct each region of America is from another. The boundary lines are almost never arbitrary; even without signs you know immediately when you have crossed into new territory. Missouri, for example, extends a long foot down into the South, between Arkansas and Kentucky, yet it is obvious at once when you enter Missouri that you are now in the Midwest, not in the South. Even the small towns somehow feel more firmly established, with the large houses heavier and more ornate in style; the streets are broad and deeply shaded by big trees; the yards are neat, green and prosperous. Farmers and gardeners are more aware of these differences and their causes than most. I asked one Missouri gardener about the land across the river in Kentucky. "Well, it's all kind of up and down, bumpylike"—he described the picturesque hills with indifference—"and sandy, thin dirt." He spat in contempt. That dirt was different from the soil here in Missouri? He looked at me in disbelief and explained with utter confidence, "This soil is the best soil on earth."

This is, of course, the premier agricultural region of the United States, and there is little in the life here that does not reflect that fact and depend upon it. This becomes most clear, unfortunately, whenever that life is threatened. Even early in the spring of 1988 the drought could be felt; the worry and frustration were palpable throughout the region. It is striking in all these thoroughly rural areas just how personal farming is. The abstract concerns about the failed harvest and increasing debt weigh heavily, of course, but it is the immediate spectacle of the parched ground and the dying plants that affects the farmers like a persistent and stabbing pain. One rainy Sunday morning in Missouri brought the first relief in months, and everyone was, even briefly, jubilant. At breakfast at Lambert's, in Sikeston, Missouri, amid portraits of mules and buckets of sorghum, glee infected everyone as the rain streamed down outside. The tables were crowded with large families of strapping individuals, three or even four generations.

Gazebo, peonies, hesperis and cars.
Mt. Gilead, Ohio, May.

"Just like a football stadium."
Tomato plants. Herman Hughes.
Sikeston, Missouri, May.

Everyone knew one another and exchanged jovial greetings and arthritis remedies; the principal topic, however, was the weather, which they were there to celebrate. As we know now, it was only a respite before the drought got much worse, but the scene made clear how all aspects of life focus on the success or failure of the farms.

Since the farms are the big focus in the Midwest, the gardens are a kind of horticultural aside. The superb soil has encouraged a rather casual approach to planting. In most parts of this country, where the soil is difficult to work, gardens are necessarily compact, no matter how much open land surrounds them; it is just too much effort to improve a large expanse for planting, and in many cases it is too expensive to haul in enough topsoil to cover a whole yard. In England, where gardening has been a national obsession for centuries, it is rare to buy property that has never been cultivated; in America it is rare to buy land that has ever felt a shovel. Simply the initial effort of cultivating a plot restricts its size. But in many parts of the Midwest the soil is almost inviting to work. A spade poked in the ground is unlikely to encounter a rock ledge, caliche, gumbo or any other variation on concrete that American gardeners call soil. As a result, plants can be stuck in anywhere, and the most common planting arrangement in the Midwest is loose groups of plants meandering across the farmyards. These yards are often not large, since farmers can be somewhat jealous of land taken out of production, but they have an expansiveness that is not found in many other parts of the country.

Out in the farmland there are not many conspicuous cottage gardens, but there are many people who grow a few favorite old-fashioned flowers in informal groups around the house or at the edges of the vegetable garden. Generations of horticultural activity are evident from the enormous peony bushes found in almost every yard. These thrive and require no effort, so they continue for decades. Iris, too, are universal. There are almost always a few roses somewhere around the house. These farmyards are seldom without a few blooms of some sort, and during the brief peony season the show across the Midwest is an unforgettable parade of these luxuriant flowers; but

Midwest favorites:
peonies and iris.
Huntington, Indiana, May.

most of the working farm families are simply too absorbed in the considerable effort of large-scale agriculture to have much time to spend on decorative garden making. Vegetable gardens, however, are universal and have their own kind of beauty. There may be thousands of acres under cultivation on every side, but it isn't the sort of agriculture that puts string beans on the table every night. It is a rare farmyard that does not have a sizable vegetable patch close to the house. This is where, in many cases, flowers find their way onto the property. A few rows of zinnias follow the early peas; a few marigolds thwart the aphids. Even without flowers, these gardens are impressive, the husky plants meticulously staked in neat rows of almost mathematical perfection. We were admiring the tomatoes in one garden, stretched on strings between silvery aged fence posts; each row was exactly two weeks ahead of its successor, the rate of growth of the graduated ranks in precise proportion. "Yes," commented the proud gardener, "it looks just like a football stadium."

You are more likely to find flower gardens in and around the towns of the Midwest than out in the countryside. Farmers who retire and move off the farms to smaller properties find that they have the time to plant for themselves. Nonfarmers, inspired by the ease with which things grow and by the spectacle of farming all around them, experiment with their own backyard agriculture.

The vast majority of cottage gardeners in this region are senior citizens. It is possible to find some younger gardeners in the large cities, many of whom create gardens in second homes outside the urban areas, but they are less likely to create gardens in the cottage style. Among the younger gardeners, meadow gardening is an increasingly popular trend, well suited to both the region and the limits of second-home horticulture. But the true cottage gardens of the Midwest are usually the creation of the older generations.

*Sedum and painted
barn. Albert Kaufman.
Huntington, Indiana, May.*

The old-fashioned perennials we saw scattered around the farmyards make up the framework of the Midwest cottage garden. These plots are not likely to feature unusual plant material. Instead, they often concentrate on a few species, but with many varieties and many plants of those species. My husband's aunt Elsie, for example, has long hybridized her own peonies, a labor requiring great patience, since a peony can take four to six years to bloom from seed. At one time she had eighty to a hundred different peony varieties, many developed by herself. Iris and day lilies similarly have their aficionados. Day lilies are popular here, as they are in the South, because they can fill a great deal of the torrid summer. Both iris and day lilies are quite easily hybridized by amateurs. Roses, too, are valued for their persistence of bloom and are seen everywhere—first the climbers and ramblers, followed by florabundas and hybrid teas. In the harsher climate of the northern Midwest shrub roses are more widely grown.

One of the greatest problems of gardening in the Midwest is the rapid movement of the seasons from very cold to very hot. The summer of 1988 was a particularly dramatic illustration of that, with stretches of ninety-degree days in mid-May that left the peonies limp after scarcely a week of bloom. And once it is hot in the Midwest, it stays hot—there is no alternation of cool evenings that gives life to many early-summer perennial species. So after the spring perennials, many gardens shift to annuals for later summer and fall bloom. Day lilies and bulb plants bridge the gap.

There could hardly have been a more difficult year than this one for seeing midwestern gardens in the middle of the season. Even the spring was somewhat sparse, but by July the drought panic had gripped almost all gardeners. Although most small backyard gardens can be watered quite economically, stringent watering restrictions hampered everyone. Most cottage gardeners are prepared to give up anything in order to water their plants, but in many areas hose and sprinkler watering was forbidden, and hauling water by hand in the hundred-degree heat was out of the question for most elderly people.

Lilies and tamarisk

in a summer of drought.

Kalamazoo, Michigan, July.

In parts of the western United States where no rainfall for six months is a fact of life year in and year out, gardens are designed with that fact in mind—a watering system is a basic design element; mulches are indispensable; techniques like trenching are an everyday essential. But the Midwest, while it does not get overabundant rainfall, expects at least enough in spring and early summer to get things growing. The leisurely sprawl of these gardens becomes a liability if hand watering is necessary.

In this drought summer only the most rugged plants were still flowering by mid-July. Many farsighted cottagers dropped their more demanding annuals early in the season and concentrated on saving major shrubs and perennials. The American natives of the prairie certainly proved their worth. The bright gold of gaillardia and rudbeckia and the majestic pink-purple heads of echinacea filled yards with color in spite of the heat and seemed to laugh at the burnt-out lawns and shriveled vegetables around them. Many members of the Compositae (daisy) family are well equipped to handle heat and dryness. The giant annual sunflower, usually a symbol of midwestern gardens, was sadly absent in many places, but the smaller ratibida or helianthus species carried the garden into the cooler fall weather. Many of our native plants have become so highly hybridized and glamorous that we fail to remember that they were originally from our harsh climate and are the plants best suited to coping with it. Our roadside black-eyed Susan went to Germany and returned as one of the most widely used perennials on the market, *Rudbeckia* 'Goldsturm.' We sometimes have to see how valued our natives are abroad before we let them into our gardens. A drought year like this one is always helpful to remind gardeners of the virtues of our tough native plants.

The mild and extended autumn in the southern Midwest allows considerable gardening late in the season. Abundant planting of a few species is again the prevailing trend. Enormous dahlias are spectacular, and a broad tapestry of chrysanthemums carpets the yards until the first black frost. Fall is also a popular planting time, as gardeners recover from the intense summer heat and start to get active again;

*Larkspur and
drumstick allium.
Chicago, Illinois, July.*

the universal array of tulips in May is the result of efforts during this pleasant season in the yard. Most hardy bulbs do well in the fertile, well-drained loam: Alliums follow the tulips in late May or June; tall and fragrant trumpet lilies are a welcome midsummer garden feature; colchicum and autumn crocus add a strange springlike touch to October. The allium species provide some of the most surprising effects in the Midwest since they are not quite traditional garden plants but somehow straddle the line between flowers and vegetables. They are easy and delightful plants of many sizes and shapes, but they are not nearly as popular as they deserve, so it was a pleasure to find them enlivening these most conservative of American gardens. Besides the amazing giant allium in Albert Kaufman's garden, we saw the midsummer drumstick allium *(A. sphaerocephalum)* punctuating a garden in Chicago and the spiky spheres of *A. christophii* rising improbably from an Indiana lawn. The Egyptian onion, with its peculiar twists and curls, is an unlikely favorite, but it appears in gardens all across the middle of America.

Not all the Midwest is as flat as the clichés tell us, but there is no denying that this region is blessed with neither interesting landforms to shape the garden nor spectacular scenery to lend it stature. The large-scale majesty of all those horizontal miles is undeniable, but it doesn't offer much to plots of under an acre. Man-made garden structures are frequently used to provide focal points—arbors or pillars for clematis or climbing roses, gazebos for outdoor seating. One ninety-year-old gardener in Ohio had her son make a charming gazebo for her garden; it was such a success he began a business of building them. But even humble sheds or barns gain importance as part of the garden scheme.

The northern Midwest is practically another climate zone. Tied by geography to the Midwest, this region looks and feels more like the cooler portions of the Northeast. Dense conifer forests replace deciduous woodland; a complex splattering of lakes and streams contrasts the broad rivers and dry plains to the south. A short, cool season of growth replaces a long, hot one. Although the American midsummer standbys—rudbeckia, echinacea, ratibida—are still prevalent, cool-

Sylvia Melchers
and Albert Kaufman;
allium in the landscape.
Huntington, Indiana, May.

weather perennials like delphinium, columbine, thalictrum and
lupine are more likely to fill the early season with splendor. The cool
evenings of this region lengthen the blooming time of most species;
the peonies, still universal spring favorites, usually last through June.
Roses are something of a gamble here, and shrubs are limited, but
this region has a more varied landscape and a cooler gardening season
conducive to work.

Overall, the gardens of the Midwest reflect on a small scale the same
approach that the farms demonstrate on a large scale. The gardeners
grow a limited number of species, and they grow them superbly, lavishly. There is little horticultural experimentation or searching for
new plants to grow. The gardens instead celebrate the familiar with
the reassuring cycle of old-fashioned flowers, as the farms follow the
cycle of planting, growing and harvest. As we saw in the summer of
1988, any cycle that depends on nature is a vulnerable one, but it is

the life to which the families of the Midwest are committed, living as they do upon the best soil on earth.

Sometimes the cottage gardens of a region present an intensified version of the garden traditions of that area. These gardens use the same flowers and express the same outlook, but in a more exaggerated form. Other cottage gardens are outstanding in a region as a wild and adventurous departure from anything around them. These gardens use radically different plant material or offer a point of view utterly distinct from their neighbors'. The garden of Albert Kaufman, outside Huntington, Indiana, is an unlikely combination of these two trends. His garden uses the same plants we saw everywhere across the Midwest and uses them in great numbers. At the same time he has a most original point of view. This garden, surrounding an old farmhouse and surrounded by miles of wheat and soybeans, is a haunting and inexplicable work of art.

Albert Kaufman's garden is clearly a fall garden; we had to be content with seeing it in May. Still, its complicated form is perhaps more apparent early in the season, before the buoyant colors of autumn distract. Hundreds of *Sedum spectabile* 'Autumn Joy' trace intricate formal patterns as delicate as lace across the flat and dusty yard. Later these designs are filled in with masses of dahlias and chrysanthemums. In May the familiar spring standbys, iris and peonies, were there in profusion, and sweet william dotted the yard with white and deep red. By far the most striking floral effect in this season was a spectacular stand of *Allium giganteum*. These enormous onions are frequently offered in catalogs, but they are frequently a disappointment since they don't return reliably every year. I have never seen such a quantity of them at once, set off brilliantly against a crimson weigela in full bloom. Mr. Kaufman appears to have a rare talent for propagation; the several thousand dahlias he plants every year have been grown from a handful he originally purchased. The same is true of all his plants.

The farm is owned by Sylvia Melchers, a sharp, vigorous woman in her seventies, scarcely taller than the giant allium in her yard. "Three hundred people came out from Huntington last fall to see this," she told us proudly. She has been at the farm a long time— "I've buried two husbands"—but the garden is a fairly recent project. Although the garden is the work of Albert Kaufman, Mrs. Melchers's enthusiasm for it is apparent. They have a working partnership of an indefinite sort. "He's no relation," Sylvia Melchers explained firmly, as if to clarify, although we hadn't asked. Their relationship is a superficial mystery compared with that presented by the garden itself, the mystery that arises from all the most imaginative and enigmatic cottage gardens. What is it these gardeners see or feel that guides them to create the work of wonder we look at laid out in the dust? Beatrice Wyatt in Ventura, Janie Porter in Mississippi, Albert Kaufman and others capture something moving and powerful in their gardens that sets them apart from those of us who simply grow plants. Perhaps we should not burden their gardens with our own complicated questions or explanations. Let us instead simply be inspired by their vision and their garden magic.

In some major cities, like Seattle, San Francisco or Los Angeles, residential areas within walking distance of downtown still have yards that can become cottage gardens. In some urban areas, however—Manhattan is an obvious example—residents can spend months without seeing a plot of real dirt. What happens to the gardening urge when it is faced with miles of asphalt and high-rise apartment buildings?

One answer is to be found in the community gardens that offer an outlet for urban gardeners. The idea of allotments, as they are usually called in Europe, is long-standing in many countries, and not just in highly urban areas. In allotments a plot of land is set apart for use by gardeners with little or no land of their own. The land is divided into small parcels and granted to workers, who usually pay a nominal fee for water and other services. These gardens may not qualify as traditional cottage gardens, since they don't accompany a house, are not the property of the gardener and in some ways may have to conform to regulations set by the community. Still, they are a wonderful demonstration of regional gardening, and they do display some of the characteristics of an American cottage garden.

Eric and Edith Sonneman began to garden in a victory garden in Chicago during World War II. Eric was an inventor of chemical formulas who had emigrated from Germany; Edith was a native midwesterner. Neither of them had ever made a garden. They answered an ad placed by a woman who was looking for participants in a victory garden on vacant land near her home. They responded out of curiosity; their benefactress arrived in a limousine and came striding across the empty lot wearing long white gloves, her chauffeur behind her carrying a shovel. On to victory!

Edith recalled, "There would be articles in the city papers, telling how to grow things. In downtown Chicago, they set up a demonstration garden; you could learn how to recognize the weeds." They continued in their first garden for years until they moved to another part of town, where they joined a community garden on the shores of Lake Michigan, near their present home. They have been gardening here more than fifteen years.

Sharing raspberries:
Edith and Eric Sonneman;
fruits of the garden.
Chicago, Illinois, July.

Although the Sonnemans have a yard around their house, it is small and shady. Besides, the community garden offers advantages beyond a thirty-by-thirty expanse in full sun. Here gardening is a form of social intercourse. The plots are cared for individually, but the broad surrounding flower borders are worked on communally by the fifty or sixty families that participate. Part of this border is a perennial planting of lilies and hosta; the rest is covered with one annual selected each year by committee. Gardeners help one another out with new projects, sharing advice and seeds. Every year part of the harvest is consumed in a grand picnic.

The plots are as diverse as the urban population of any major American city. In some only vegetables are grown, or just one vegetable; the Sonnemans' Mexican neighbors grow only tomatillos for salsa. Eric and Edith grow a typical cottage mixture of edibles and ornamentals. All the land was reclaimed from the lake, so the heavy clay soil needs plenty of work, but the cool waterside breeze makes gardening pleasant even through Chicago's typically torrid summers.

There are some disadvantages to the public nature of the garden. "Yes," said Edith, "it's a little discouraging; people come through and take things, but usually only big things, like onions. It's too much work for them to pick the spinach."

"Aren't you going to ask the sixty-four-dollar question: Why do I garden?" Eric Sonneman, an articulate and thoughtful man, expressed his own feelings on the subject and speaks, I believe, for many gardeners who are not so able to put their ideas into words: "When I was a child, I wanted to go to the moon. A fantastic idea. But when the Apollo mission took off, I had played a part in it. [His antifriction chemical coating was used on the spacecraft.] In a smaller way, gardening is the realization of your dreams. It is a way of making your future real. You must work at it, and work hard, but if you do really work, you can achieve what you want." He may have been thinking of his daughter Eve and her photographs when he added, "It is a little like what we expect of our children."

The West ❦ Texas

There is enough of Texas to fill all the clichés you've heard about it. What's left after that would still make a big state. All the soap opera stereotypes are there, and the lingering shades of J. Frank Dobie fight it out with the more recent visions of Louis Lamour and Larry McMurtry. It doesn't matter which version you believe; there is always more of Texas to surprise.

Coastal Houston and its environs are linked by both geography and climate to the South. (By economy, too; the recent oil crises have hurt Mississippi and Louisiana almost more than Texas.) The humidity is high; the soil is close to neutral. Even though there is a great deal about the outlook of this area that makes it clearly Texan, some of the languor of the South remains, and the azaleas to go with it. But head out into the center of Texas, and it is obvious that you are not merely going west; you are entering the West. The towns are smaller and more firmly defined by the ever-increasing spaces between them. The humidity drops; the pH rises. The landscape changes in both subtle and outlandish ways, but the result is consistent: This doesn't look like any place you have been before. The improbable landscapes are the hallmark of the West. The spaces are overwhelming, intimidating, and the natural life that is evident here, while dramatic, is not designed to make anyone feel at home.

But in the midst of all that, the hill country of central Texas is another kind of surprise. Although it is impossible ever to lose the sense that Texas is endless, the landscape here is intimate, inviting, unexpectedly small-scale. Low, rhythmic swells of land are lightly shaded by short, sparse trees. Under this delicate canopy and covering the rolling pastures and grasslands are some of the most spectacular wildflowers in our country. It doesn't matter how many posters or calendars you have seen; the first view of a field of bluebonnets and paintbrush is heart-stopping. Texas, unlike many parts of America, has made a considerable effort to make this natural beauty accessible.

Raised beds.
Mike Schroeder.
San Antonio, Texas, April.

Sweet peas and amaryllis.
San Antonio, Texas, April.

The Texas Department of Highways has taken major steps to protect and enhance the roadside flowers throughout the state. The Wildflower Research Center, near Austin, is concerned with wildflowers in all parts of America, but not surprisingly, it has done a great deal of its work with Texas natives. The efforts of these organizations, although highly laudable, would be irrelevant to our book if the wildflowers of Texas simply stayed wild. But in Texas, more than in any part of our country, wildflowers are having an enormous effect on the American cottage garden.

Texas may not be the most difficult state in which to garden, but that doesn't mean it is easy. Along the moist and moderate Gulf Coast, gardeners flirt with semitropical possibilities, but inland regions don't dare. The summer temperatures of ninety or a hundred would make anyone think tropical, but winter temperatures frequently hover in the twenties, and your jungle could turn black overnight. Soil difficulties are another headache. Most soil here is very alkaline, and a great deal of it is sticky, impermeable clay, the most extreme form of which is called caliche. Backbreaking labor and desperate ingenuity are often both needed to garden in this kind of ground. Container gardening is one limited solution, often used for rose bushes; topsoil is sometimes brought in for raised beds above the clay. One solution to both the climate and the soil problems is the use of native plants.

One reason I think the native plant approach has caught on with such force here lies in the basic Texas outlook. Independence is the keynote of Texas life, and it shapes the gardens as well as everything else. There is a real delight in all things authentically Texan, including native plants. Gardeners here have little interest in classic garden traditions. Their approach is original and energetic; their gardens are brave, eccentric and exciting.

Texas wildflowers are not necessarily easy to grow—the bluebonnet is notoriously unaccommodating, even on its home ground—but there is great diversity among the natives, and big groups such as salvia, penstemon or oenothera are amenable to cultivation. Some of these are simply grown in the garden with familiar cultivated species like sweet peas, roses, amaryllis or larkspur; in other gardens, wild-

The Latin influence.
San Antonio, Texas, April.

flower mixtures are used to turn parts of a plot into a slice of prairie. It is delightful to find these miniature meadows used instead of traditional lawns, shrubs and bedding plants. The lawn has not yet lost its stranglehold, but even modern office buildings are trying alternatives borrowed from the roadside and the backyard.

Hispanic culture is another strong influence on Texas gardening. The gardeners of Mexico and other countries of Latin America contribute both plants and style to the American *mezcla*. Many Latin gardeners have an attitude oddly similar in one way to the English: They simply can't imagine life without a garden. Their similarity to the English stops there—they favor brilliant colors piled atop one another, and the Latin concept of order might make an Englishman blanch—but they bring gaiety and a great deal of knowledge to gardening in the Southwest. Many plants that thrive in Latin America can survive in Texas; adventurous plantsmen are making an effort to bring these plants into wider circulation.

After the many surprises of Texas, the diversity among gardeners is almost to be expected. There are many young gardeners here. "Young" for a gardener is generally anyone under fifty, but here there are enthusiasts in their twenties or thirties. The young gardeners here start out with a lack of preconceived notions about the garden they want to make—a refreshing change after some of the resolute garden trendiness to be found on either coast of America. Lucinda Hutson, a young writer and accomplished chef, grows an incredible array of herbs in her small Austin plot; she experiments with many Mexican culinary plants, including yerbanise *(Tagetes lucida)*, the Mexican substitute for tarragon, and hoya santa, an enormous leaf that smells like root beer and is used to wrap tamales. There are also many who have been gardening here for fifty or sixty years: M. W. Carlton, who is eighty-eight, has been experimenting with Texas native plants for the last four decades. His farm in Lockhart is a wild mixture of meadow and cottage garden; his yard sparkles with *Linum rigidum* and callirhoe, while the rare golden-show sprouts from old milk jugs and coffee tins. On his property in mid-April over 150 species of native plants can be observed.

Ready to plant.
Julia Villanueva
and chrysanthemums.
San Marcos, Texas, April.

One unexpected aspect of Texas gardening is the considerable botanical and horticultural information possessed by many of the gardeners. As we have seen, this is not really necessary for making a lovely garden; many of the gardens in this book were created by people who had not the slightest interest in the names of the plants they grow. But in Texas gardeners are prepared to call a salvia a salvia, then tell you its name in English and Spanish as well. Plant societies are popular here, as are classes in horticulture. Many of the radio stations carry gardening talk and call-in programs; a particularly fine one in San Antonio has a wide and vocal following. All these elements contribute to the general sense you find in Texas that gardening is important—not just a slightly mad pursuit of eccentrics, but an occupation with meaning, producing a beauty to be shared by everyone.

Most Texas gardeners don't try to defy their summer climate. Even in April afternoons were in the nineties, and most gardeners admitted that in a few weeks the garden would be over. The ubiquitous roses erupt periodically during the summer, and some of the tough warm-climate bulbs persist, but most gardening subsides until the cool fall and early spring. This midsummer dormancy, besides being essential to the comfort of the gardeners, is necessary for the survival of many of the native plants, which are accustomed to drought during the summer months. Because of this estivation, the gardens here are seldom luxuriant in the way of more tropical settings; the plant material doesn't have the lush expanse of surface made possible by rainfall and high humidity. This doesn't mean that the gardens are severe. The abundant assortment of species provides endless new plant combinations; an invigorating creativity sets these gardens apart. The independence and originality of the gardens here make them perfectly Texan.

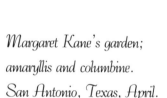

Margaret Kane's garden;
amaryllis and columbine.
San Antonio, Texas, April.

Margaret Kane, in San Antonio, seems like the most typical of cottage gardeners, with her small yard overflowing with flowers. She is seventy-five and has been cultivating the same garden for more than fifty years. Her knowledge of plants is humbling; she probably has not forgotten a plant name in the entire time she has been gardening. She is an active member of several plant societies and she regularly donates plants for sales at the botanical garden. Bulbs are a particular interest. Besides superb examples of familiar iris and amaryllis, she has many rare species; lapeirousia, brought to a friend in Florida by a missionary from South Africa, has made its way through Texas because of the efforts of this remarkable woman.

An enormous variegated crinum occupied most of a small shed in
which slightly tender species spend the winter. Along the side of the
house we were riveted by *Amorphophallus Rivieri*, a huge, nearly
black calla-like cup. Mrs. Kane admits her garden had a big advantage with naturally rich loam soil and good shade—necessary protection from the powerful Texas sun. She grows many Texas natives but
is no purist: "I don't really care if a plant is native or not, as long as
it blooms." Her garden is a perfect blend of comfort and interest;
the rare species mix with the familiar and don't distract from the
coherence developed by long experience and a practiced eye.

Scott Ogden and echeveria; suburban melee. New Braunfels, Texas, April.

In a recently developed subdivision outside New Braunfels, a garden shatters the quiet and sterile suburban landscape. This isn't a meadow in the front yard; it's a melee. Violent spears of *Gladiolus byzantinus* wave above a cloud of salvia and delphinium. Giant fossils and children's toys line the driveway, along with an occasional ferocious horse-crippler cactus. Scott Ogden, a tall and enthusiastic Texan, is dazzling us with a combination of charm and formidable botanical nomenclature. He has a flair for Latin binomials and a fascination with systematic botany that is wasted on much of his day-to-day life. Ogden works in the world of horticulture—he is a salesman for a nursery wholesaler—but he admits that when he's working, taxonomy is irrelevant. "Everyone just says, 'I want ten of the round ones and ten with points,'" when ordering the usual foundation shrubs. That kind of cliché planting hasn't touched his half acre. Instead, a

collection of snake plants (genus *Manfreda*) occupies a prominent corner; these are fascinating rosettes of striped or spotted leaves with wands of barely visible and occasionally foul-smelling flowers. All the warm-climate bulbs are here: many varieties of amaryllis and huge crinum for opulent summer bloom; vivid red yucca-like hesper-aloe, an exciting native; asphodel, iris, *Ornithogallum nabonense* and *Scilla hyacinthoides*. Armed with excellent Spanish, Scott Ogden combs the mountains of Mexico for new species to try. Back in New Braunfels, he eyes abandoned properties for old garden plants. He also seeks out older gardeners with knowledge and plants to share; his lapeirousia came from Margaret Kane. Scott Ogden makes gardening into an utterly absorbing adventure—and great fun. He presented each of us with a twenty-pound fossil shell. "Don't forget," he reminded us as we left. "That's *Exogyra ponderosa*."

The West ❦ *Utah* ❧ *Montana* ❦ *Wyoming*

The mountains around Salt Lake City as we prepare to land are blue and one-dimensional in a faint haze, stark and schematic as painted theater sets. The brilliant, still surface of the lake below is equally without life, the opposite of water, with only desolation at its edges. In Billings, Montana, the plane lands on a red tablelike plateau that drops sharply down several stories of rimrock; the small city lies on the flat plain below. Between these cosmopolitan centers and around them in every direction is the dramatic and limitless scenery of the western frontier, as unfamiliar as another planet. This is the stuff of myth, as well as the background of everyday hardship. We saw the millions of black and still-burning acres of Yellowstone smoking and smoldering beneath the plane. You scarcely need such violent reminders of the closeness of unpredictable nature when you are in the West, but they are everywhere.

This is magnificent country, invigorating and alluring but offering a life of great risks and narrow margins. One response to the challenge of survival on the frontier is the creation of a highly directed society, insular and tightly controlled, standing against the elements. The opposite is also found here: the reckless and independent individual who stakes his flexibility and ingenuity against the odds and manages somehow to survive. Melodramatic alternatives, perhaps, but the exaggeration of melodrama seems natural here. These radically dif-ferent approaches to life can be found side by side in the West, and they are reflected in the American cottage garden.

Utah was not the first state in America founded by and for a reli-gious sect, but it is virtually the only state today that presents a homogeneous religious outlook. Members of the Church of Jesus Christ of Latter-day Saints, popularly called Mormons, make up roughly 56 percent of the population of the state of Utah; they are not an overwhelming majority in all the major cities—in Salt Lake, they are only about 48 percent of the population—but in some areas they can account for up to 90 percent of the populace.

Exuberance in August: gypsophila,
marigolds, phlox. Salt Lake City, Utah.

Mallow in the
conifers. John English.
Salt Lake City, Utah, August.

Do these demographics have anything to do with gardening? Absolutely. As we have seen, religious belief and gardening function side by side in many of the gardeners we met throughout the country, and it is a natural combination, but until I got to Utah, I had never heard of an organized religion that urged its followers to get out and garden. One of the first directives from the Almighty, as passed along by Brigham Young, was to make the ground fruitful. For the Mormons, arriving after months of difficult travel to find a barren, dry and alkaline plain, this advice may have been superfluous. But they faced the challenge; the energy and organization of these people are formidable, and no one visiting Salt Lake City today can doubt that this is a society that can make something grow anywhere.

Extreme aridity and alkaline soil are the familiar western conditions from Brigham Young's day to the present. Irrigation is essential, since virtually no rain falls from May to October; water comes from wells, springs or runoff from the nearby mountains. The worst of the soil here is very fine clay appropriately called gumbo. Black, sticky, intractable, it requires years of sand-and-compost treatment to make it productive. Many gardeners give up and haul in topsoil by the truckload. In spite of these drawbacks, the yards and gardens of Salt Lake are extensive and lush. Lawns seem as necessary to life as indoor plumbing, to judge from the effort and water expended on them. Big backyard vegetable gardens are the rule. Mormons are encouraged to have a year's supply of food stored in their houses at all times, and much of that is home-grown and preserved. Annuals of all kinds are often stuck in the vegetable rows, too, particularly gladiolus, which many people hybridize as a hobby.

I am not sure that Brigham Young said anything in particular about the religious importance of petunias, but they are clearly the annual of choice. (One doctor was spending $750 every year on petunias for the front of his house before he switched to dwarf conifers.) This is a perfect climate for many annuals as long as they can be watered.

*Perfect order; garden
of Mr. and Mrs. Sudbury.
Salt Lake City, Utah, August.*

Even if you don't like petunias, you have to admire how they are
grown here: Rich billows of color line walks, surround trees, make
foundation plantings and everywhere offer a vibrant contrast with the
deep green lawns.

Perennials do surprisingly well in this climate (or series of climates;
just in Salt Lake, the climate can range from temperate Zone 6 to
Zone 2 or 3 up in the nearby mountains), but they are only slowly
becoming more widely used, and in general they are most often
grown by non-Mormon gardeners. The same is true of native plants.
Some natives, like the ebullient helianthus seen everywhere, are simply weeds that provide color and are tolerated during the slow periods
of late summer; the more fascinating and difficult species are ignored
by all except the most adventurous and sophisticated, although cactus
and succulents are quite popular.

Because of the connection made in the minds of many Mormons between cultivation and salvation, the gardens here come to represent a state of grace: Part of the beauty of a garden is the triumph of man over hostile nature. This is why the gardens here are such a stunning contrast with the land around them. These immaculate lawns and vibrant annuals turn away from the harsh, dramatic scenery on all sides and emphasize the power of man. One reason bedding plants are so popular is that they respond to careful management by behaving in a completely predictable fashion; when they are finished, everything can be cleared out and a clean slate prepared for next season. Perennials are a little too haphazard to satisfy the majority, and they don't provide the ceaseless production so gratifying to the lover of petunias. Perennials go out of bloom; they spread in unpredictable ways, and they often defy the nicely symmetrical plan of the Mormon plot. There are beautiful perennial gardens in Salt Lake, and there are wild and eccentric mixtures of plants, but these are not gardens characteristic of the Latter-day Saints.

Out in Montana, George Gee.
Roscoe, Montana, August.

The gardens in Utah present an interesting reflection of the people who make them: conservative, meticulously planned and maintained, highly controlled, demanding a great deal of time and attention and returning a great deal in exchange. The eager demand for plants in this region has encouraged excellent nurseries and plant centers which sell a great deal more than petunias. There is, overall in Utah, a knowledgeable enthusiasm for gardening that is expressed in all segments of the population. Because of the flowery examples presented by the Latter-day Saints, there are many converts to gardening here. It may be one of their most effective forms of proselytizing.

Even in downtown Salt Lake City you can never lose sight of the mountains. The Wasatch range on one side and the Oquirrhs on the other enclose the city in a bowl; it is a matter of minutes to reach the nearest foothills. The forces of nature are seldom forgotten for long. Only a few years ago floods raced through the main streets of town and continued to flow for weeks. But the homogeneous social and religious beliefs so evident here create a strong sense of unity and protection. There is the firm belief that God is on the side of the settlers and will, eventually, prevail.

In the vast spaces of Montana, Wyoming or the Dakotas, it's much less clear which side God is on; the Almighty is as distant, as impartial and as limitless as the big sky for which this region is named. Here, as in Texas, independence is the foundation of the rugged, lonely and exhilarating life of the range. The indigenous architecture is a perfect mirror of the desire to be alone. Even on large and prosperous ranches, there is seldom one great house, regardless of the number of people. Instead, settlements of individual log cabins are the rule, as if each separate room needed open space around it. These beautiful small buildings cluster like mushrooms along the creeks or springs in the valleys, while the thousands of acres of grazing land run up the slopes of the mountains in every direction. The flatland in the valleys is irrigated for hay (an astonishing idea to

Delphinium and
tiger lilies. George Gee.
Roscoe, Montana, August.

someone from the East, where any farmer with an acre flat enough to mow accepts two cuttings a year as his natural right). As in Utah, everything is grown with irrigation, but surprisingly this does not always confine the garden to a single plot. Often the flowers seem as bent on independence as the buildings, so separate plots accompany each of several buildings or trace an informal path between them.

The climate here is as rugged as the terrain, but it sounds more difficult and limiting than it turns out to be. The growing season is short: Memorial Day to Labor Day in a good year, mid-June to mid-August in an average one; practically everyone can recall a heavy mid-June snowfall during his lifetime. At the higher elevations, of course, everything is exaggerated, and frost can be expected at almost any time. But brilliant, virtually unlimited sunshine and very long days seem to overcome the brevity of the season. Warm days and cool nights satisfy a wide variety of both annuals and perennials. Low humidity makes disease and fungus practically unknown; one long-time gardener had never seen mildew before the great heat and humidity of the summer of '88. The winters are very cold but relatively dry and with excellent snow cover in most places; many perennials that are not hardy in the Northeast can winter over here.

The garden flowers grown in this part of the country are a surprising and diverse assortment, and this diversity is increasing rapidly. Gardening here is greatly on the rise, and there are few preconceived ideas about what can or should be grown, so almost anything is tried. This is certainly the right approach, considering how little we actually know about the hardiness of plants or the complex equations of climate. I would not have been able to predict some of the outstanding successes in gardens here. Why are snapdragons such a triumph all through the West, wintering over, self-sowing and generally making themselves at home? The western annuals, not surprisingly, are spectacular: clarkia in loose, sprawling garlands of rich color; startling blue phaecelia; godetia of deep red and salmon satin. Many of the classic perennials could rival those grown in the Pacific Northwest. Hollyhocks and delphinium nonchalantly top eight or nine

Ten thousand gladioli.
Dave Wasden.
Cody, Wyoming, August.

feet; gypsophila drowns the border in a froth of white. As we have seen, there are bulbs for every region of America, no matter how difficult; here the enchanting native calochortus arouses the envy of gardeners from either coast. But even the familiar tulip offers a pleasant surprise; in the dry, alkaline soil of this region, most tulips will return for years, especially if they are planted where they receive little summer water.

According to most of the hardiness maps, much of this region is Zone 3 or less, but from seeing the gardens, you are made to wonder about the accuracy of the whole system. There is no doubt that many parts of the Rockies and the high western plains have winters with temperatures firmly fixed at minus twenty, but then why does gypsophila die in Utica, New York, but not in Billings, Montana? It is true that woody plant material is much more limited here, so ornamental trees and shrubs don't play a great part in most gardens. The tough and alkaline-loving lilac is one on which gardeners can depend; likewise the hardy olive trees (*Eleagnus* species), which have naturalized here. In the wild, few trees are apparent; willow and poplar congregate along the creek sides, but only the native spruces venture up the slopes.

But the absence of larger plant material is hardly noticed in the broad and colorful selection of annuals, bulbs and herbaceous plants that is just beginning to be known to gardeners in this region. One consistent interest throughout the area is plants for drying. The parched summer and low humidity make harvesting and drying very easy, and there are beautiful wild plants that can contribute to dried arrangements. With such a short season of fresh flowers (and such uninspired and expensive florist material during the long winter), this is a natural pursuit. Strawflowers and everlastings such as xeranthemum, gomphrena, helichrysum or ammobium are commonly seen, although seldom pronounced; they produce lavishly, much better than they do in the East, in general.

Ranch house
and wildflowers.
Lynn Selby.
Cody, Wyoming,
August.

Herbs are another unexpected interest. The cuisine throughout the region is far from sophisticated or trendy, so the prevalence of basil, thyme, lovage, savory and borage is something of a mystery, although they grow extremely well here. I noticed big clumps of basil in the garden of one longtime rancher, and I asked him what he did with it. "I like to rub it on my steak" was his explanation, although he also said it was nice to have a bit of it in his pocket.

As I mentioned above, everything is grown with irrigation, but this brief phrase may not convey what an enormous part watering plays in the lives of western gardeners. Even with a complicated system of built-in pipes, tubes, spray heads or trickles with computerized timers, watering demands time, attention and money throughout the entire season. One gardener admitted that the monthly water bill was considerably over one hundred dollars a month. "But this is what we like to do," she explained. "And we can't go away, not even for a day. But we don't want to go anywhere." That is the perfect summary of the cottage gardener's frame of mind. Because the climate in the high plains, or in most of the other western climates, assumes no rain will fall for months, watering practices are part of the established routine of gardening; in a summer when most of the country suffered from severe drought, this region showed it less than any, because drought is so often the ordinary state of things. Gardeners who rely on natural rainfall completely, as they do in the Southeast or parts of the Midwest, were much less prepared to cope.

Out in the ample yards of the ranches we saw loose plantings in informal groups, but even in the more confined spaces of the towns gardens are far from regimented. They are usually fenced in some way, however, particularly if there is anything edible; varmints are not underestimated in this part of the country. Moose and bears in the backyard are an inescapable reminder that this is still the frontier. And it is the frontier of gardening as well, where each yard suggests a new approach, each collection of plants presents unexpected ideas; where every planting season brings discoveries; where each gardener, with the independent spirit of the West, goes out to create the garden only he has in mind.

Jessica and Dean Smith and scarecrow; grapevine and amaranth. Billings, Montana, August.

The home of Jessica and Dean Smith is right in Billings, minutes from the airport, but it looks like a frontier outpost—a low, sprawling log building with a stockade fence. Jessica grew up in the sheltering Polish community around Boston; she had never been outside it until she moved west with her first husband to a tiny town on the Blackfoot reservation near Glacier National Park. She speaks with great cheerfulness now of the miseries of the early days: "It was so terrible; I cried for years. It was always cold; nothing grew there. It could snow in July. The wind was so fierce the children walked backwards to school." This resourceful woman made the best of it by learning to paint and practicing a variety of crafts. Jessica moved to Billings with her five daughters after the death of her husband and started to make a new life as an artist. "It isn't easy to sell Impressionism in Montana; people say, 'She doesn't do too bad for someone who can't draw.'" In spite of the absence of cowboys and Indians, her paintings now sell very well, as do her exquisite handcrafted dolls.

Jessica and Dean met and married ten years ago. "We decided we needed a project to share. So we started a garden." They have had the garden five years now, and much of the planting is still experimental. "Oh, we'll try anything." Dried flowers are particularly evident late in the season: Long, hanging burgundy amaranth sweeps to the ground; huge plants of bells of Ireland are almost three feet high.

Their garden has the flavor and charm of a folk art quilt, set in squares, each with one or two strong colors, then an edge of vegetables or herbs, then some rows of everlastings, another brilliant square of annuals (four-o'clocks and zinnias against the red wall of the shed), an inviting lodgepole arbor with several kinds of vines, a tall stand of sunflowers towering over the celosia, a corner of cosmos for the scarecrow—enormous variety carefully ordered but always lively, unexpected and full of humor. It is a fresh and personal garden-in-progress, alive with the energy and openhearted warmth of the two artists who are creating it.

The Northeast ✿ *New England*

We have shown cottage gardens of great diversity from many parts of the United States, yet whenever I mention the term "cottage garden" to people, no matter where they live, the image they have is always the same: a New England saltbox surrounded by hollyhocks and roses enclosed by a picket fence. And in New England, more than anywhere else, the gardens conform to our expectations: They are created within definite limits; they are perfectly managed; they are exquisitely traditional. They seem to match most closely our ideas of an English cottage garden. Yet like the Yankees who make them, they are more complicated and original than they first appear.

There is no question of the role of boundaries in the New England garden. Nature has created undeniable constraints, and the society of man has reinforced them. The first, most noticeable restraining influence on New England gardens is the climate. The summers are short and erratic in their distribution of temperature and rainfall. Some years the growing season is almost like that of England (except for being three months shorter), with cool temperatures and plentiful rain; other years the yards are parched or smothered by blankets of hot and humid air. It is almost unnecessary to describe the winters, since they are the standard against which all terrible weather is judged. It was fascinating but not too surprising to find that even the harsh winters of the northern Rockies are, in some ways, easier to bear than those of New England; many plants that will not survive in interior Vermont flourish in Montana.

The landforms of New England also pose limitations. Early settlers struggled to claim small farms from the dense forest, but with the decline of agriculture in this region in the last century, the forest has swept back in around the homesteads. The dramatic ups and downs of the landscape compress house and garden sites. The omnipresent New England rock dulls shovels and enthusiasm in equal measure. Of course, these limitations are also frequently advantages.

Climbing hydrangea.
Clinton, Connecticut, July.

Maltese cross with foxglove,
plume poppy and baptisia.
Charlestown, Rhode Island, July.

The woodlands provide privacy in a densely populated area and have contributed to the development of sophisticated shady wildflower gardens. The abrupt rises and falls add enormous interest to even a tiny plot and help increase drainage in a region that can certainly use it. The endless rock creates spectacular natural effects, builds walls and makes paving and has fostered an interest in rock gardening that has greatly broadened the range of plants grown here.

Coastal New England has a milder version of the climate, but there are still many factors that confine the size of the properties. These have always been highly populated shores and are only becoming more so. Many of the coastal New England towns are perched on extremely rocky waterfronts where only the most compact plantings could fit, not to say survive. And here, instead of blizzards, gardeners deal with salt spray and the inundations of hurricanes. All this contributes to tiny and intensely planted plots.

There is the question of why anyone would try to garden here in the first place; at least part of the answer must lie with the New England love of history and tradition. The early settlers had little choice but to garden, and the English yeomen who first tried to plow these acres always left a corner for household herbs and decorative plants. Many of the plants of England would not live here, but some would and still do. The plants of the New World were a terrific adventure, and still are. Much of the landscape was not the sort that would lend itself to extensive formal gardens, but most of the people who came here to make their homes had not lived in that kind of setting in England either. So the little, huddled houses were joined by small, tightly enclosed gardens. Fences provided some protection for the plants, both from the weather and from human and animal pilfering; they do the same today. And remember that this is the country where "good fences make good neighbors." The Yankee still prefers to have boundaries made explicit, and there is little quibbling about a stone wall. This is the only part of America where the gardens are more often fenced than not. But even properties that are not visibly enclosed give a strong impression of being contained, if only by the shape of the landscape or the character of the gardener.

Baby's breath.
Charlestown, Rhode
Island, July.

Gardens are, of course, extremely perishable, so it would be unrealistic to suppose that even a fraction of the gardens of the seventeenth century made their way down to the present. What they did was to establish a tradition of small decorative gardens in scale with the historic houses and plots. There have been periods of very elaborate garden design in New England, but vast estate gardens managed by troops of retainers are much more susceptible to economic change; few gardens from the so-called Golden Age at the turn of the century survive today, simply because they were not gardens that people could make for themselves. Today there is an enormous upsurge in gardening in this region, and the gardens people are going back to for models are the tiny cottage plots of the earliest settlers.

There is more to the New England cottage gardens than simply their long history, although that alone would set them apart from most gardens in this country. What makes them particularly intriguing is the interplay of a confined form and an unexpectedly adventurous content. Considering the climate, it is surprising how many things will grow here, and there has been an enormous increase in the range of plants available just in the last decade. Some of this is the result of active groups like the American Rock Garden Society or the native plant societies, which have energetic members in this area. Although these organizations and the plants they espouse may appeal to a fairly select following, their efforts have made interesting plant material more widely known and sought after by the general gardener.

The Yankee entrepreneurial spirit has also contributed to the current New England garden explosion. Many avid gardeners have decided that the best way to deal with excess plants is to sell them; New England is now dotted with tiny one- and two-person nurseries that developed out of a backyard hobby. It is likely that many of these businesses are borderline when it comes to profit, but they are hugely successful in disseminating new plants and arousing garden interest.

Teasel and artemesia.

The Allagash, Maine,

August.

(Vermont provides a list of some of its plant-selling gardens—a great shortcut for visitors looking for cottage gardens in that state.) So the traditional-looking front yard of that New England saltbox may very well have ten species of veronica amid the hollyhocks and draba and dracocephalum along with the daffodils.

The old-fashioned garden favorites are not abandoned. Perennials predominate and include all the most cold-resistant English cottage classics, but hardy annuals like larkspur, calendula and poppies fill up the corners; along the coast annuals play a greater part. The hybrid tea rose is not so much in evidence because of its dubious hardiness here, but ramblers, climbers and shrubs have an important place, particularly along the shore, where the glorious wild beach roses paint the landscape with pale or shocking pink in late June. Native plants in general are increasingly popular; some of the most beautiful are woodland shade lovers, but even some of these find their way into the darker corners of the cottage plot. Colorful monarda and *Asclepias tuberosa* are natural choices for sunnier exposures.

Each New England state has its own specific gardening personality, and among these Rhode Island has one of the most unexpected. Although surrounded by rocks on every side, much of this tiny state consists of flat and comparatively rich farmland. Many of the farms are now abandoned, but the good soil and mild coastal weather encourage lush planting by the latest wave of gardening settlers. Interior Maine is another world unto itself, a superb isolated wilderness which exaggerates both the harshness and the beauty of the New England climate. The gardens here are wilder, more idiosyncratic, less contained in form but more limited in content. Even far up into the Allagash, the New England garden tradition persists, defying the short season and the rugged land. Brilliant in their late-season glory, these patches of color are the last flashes of cultivation before the trackless northern woods—and the endless Maine winter—close in.

*Edmond L. Emery;
hand-hewn gate. Clinton,
Connecticut, July.*

Mr. Emery's garden on Main Street in Clinton, Connecticut, seems
as much a part of the town as the tall white Presbyterian church on
the village green. I remember this garden from years ago on our
annual family trips to the shore; my mother, who spent her child-
hood here, remembers it from much longer ago than I do. Edmond
L. Emery was a schoolteacher and private tutor, but now he is retired
and has more time for his true vocation, gardening. "I've gardened
all my life," he says simply; his garden has the rich and finely
detailed beauty that results only from decades of work. His father
was a landscape gardener and florist, so Edmond Emery had an early
education in the basic points of cultivation and construction; he
made all the wonderful rough-wood fences, arbors and gates himself.

The property surrounding the 1720 house is surprisingly extensive
for a yard right in town. Mr. Emery has divided the land with graceful high fences hung with grapevines, so the large vegetable plot
seems very distant from the rock plantings or the beds of perennials.
The whole yard is enclosed in lavish swaths of the native beach ram-
bler, which shield it from the clamor of Route 1, only a few feet
away. The plant material here is not unusual, and everything fits
together with a quiet harmony. The broad, snowy flowers of a white
clematis twine across the clothesline; glistening trumpet lilies broad-
cast their fragrance in front of a wall of grapes. Self-sown larkspurs
thread the rose garlands with purple. Inside the fence you are in a
world of timeless and contemplative industry as Edmond L. Emery
perfects his work of a lifetime.

The Northeast & The Middle Atlantic States

The mild climate of the Mid-Atlantic States seems like a gardening paradise after the rigors of New England. Why is it, then, that cottage gardens seem so hard to find here? The simplest answer is: because of the suburbs. The small towns and smaller yards of New England created an irresistible setting for compressed but extravagant planting in spite of the climate. But most communities throughout New Jersey, Long Island or Pennsylvania are not set up that way. Whether a suburb consists of tract housing on quarter-acre treeless lots or the palatial "estate" developments with two acres of stylized landscaping, suburban life stifles the urge for creative gardening. The owners of these houses are often young families of commuters with little time to devote to a garden. The size of the lots, too, is discouraging: too small for privacy, but too big to provide the compressed space that lends itself to all-out planting. An even more fundamental cause of this bleak landscape is simply peer pressure. Lawns, shrubs and foundation plantings are seen as the limits of outdoor life; only a real radical would have a plot of tomatoes hidden behind the house. Anything as flamboyant as a gladiolus is greeted with a shudder. "Good taste" in the suburbs frowns on the vibrant, the disorganized or the personal forms of gardening. Some of this does seem to be changing in the recent surge of garden interest, and there have always been exceptions tucked away here and there (my father has confounded convention for years with his masses of flowers). But the suburbs continue to be the hardest place to find wild and wonderful displays of bloom. Small towns and even quite urban areas have more to offer of garden interest.

In many parts of the country we have seen the contributions of different ethnic groups: In California, Texas and the Southwest, the Latin spirit dominates many areas and offers much to cottage culture; in parts of the Midwest, German and Scandinavian garden traditions have dictated plant selection and ordered the yards.

The Italian influence.
Millburn, New Jersey,
September.

Tomatoes and figs.
Short Hills, New
Jersey, September.

Throughout the Middle Atlantic States, it is the Italian influence that stamps the most arresting cottage gardens and brings life and color into the midst of sedate suburban green. There are Italian gardeners all over our country, but here in a climate well suited to them, the Italians seem to thrive, and they stand out particularly for their indifference to suburban conventions. Only an Italian would have an arbor of grapes and gourds in the center of posh Short Hills, New Jersey; basil, parsley, pumpkins and tomatoes instead of pachysandra and hosta cover his tiny yard. Only an Italian would nurture a fig tree in northern New Jersey; we found two of them in gardens within half a mile of each other. (However mild New Jersey is compared with other states, there is still much too much hard freezing through the winter for a fig. These trees are lovingly cut back and laboriously wrapped late each fall. The effort is well worth it; we ended our garden visits sticky and stuffed with fresh fruit.)

Italian cottage gardens share many of the characteristics we have seen in small non-Italian gardens across the country, but there are a few noticeable features that set them apart. These gardens are marked by a combination of formality and exuberance that descends in a direct line from the Villa d'Este to Secaucus. The Italians are masters of plant manipulation, and their gardens abound with pleaching, pollarding and espalier. Pot culture also shows the Italians' appreciation of the sculptural possibilities of plants; herbs and shrubs are often trained as standards in pots. Pruning is an art form for Italian gardeners. On the other hand, they take a distinctly casual approach to garden structure and materials; an elaborately trimmed bay tree or oleander is as likely to be in a truck tire as in a terra-cotta pot. Vegetables and herbs are of primary interest, and flowers and edibles mix freely in the beds. Rare is the Italian garden without some form of outdoor seating, usually set up for meals. Inviting arbors of grape are most common, but occasionally a bower of trained fruit trees provides shelter for a table and chairs.

Birdhouse and fall flowers:
chrysanthemums, celosia.
Clayton, Delaware, October.

Italian gardeners, like Latin gardeners in Texas or Los Angeles, are frequently found close together in neighborhoods within a city or town. In Philadelphia a knot of Italian plant lovers forms a lively string of backyards interwoven with shared plants. In Clearfield, Pennsylvania, one whole end of town seems to be settled with Italian gardeners; virtually every yard has a vegetable plot of some kind. One elderly gardener showed us through her own yard and a neighbor's while reciting some of the mouth-watering recipes "from the old country" she was looking forward to: eggplant stuffed with mint; zucchini and walnuts; ten variations on a tomato. It was a surprise to find burdocks flourishing next to the peonies and grapes until she explained how you can blanch them, pickle them and eat them cold; nothing is wasted in the Italian garden.

The Italian delights in the odd and fantastic footnotes of the plant world: a gourd five feet long, a squash that resembles an Elizabethan hat, gigantic celosias like huge red velvet brains. Annuals are much more common than perennials in these gardens since flowers and vegetables are all usually grown together, then turned over fresh in the spring. Because of the long, mild autumn in the Mid-Atlantic States, this season offers a particularly rich display of colorful confusion, with giant dahlias, asters and chrysanthemums among the late pumpkins and squash.

Not all the cottage gardeners of this region are Italian, of course. This just seems an appropriate place to examine a prominent strain of ethnic garden style. The gracious coastal climate of these states encourages many forms of gardening once you escape the most suburban areas. Delaware is long accustomed to being overlooked, but its quiet towns and serene landscapes have abundant appealing gardens. The Delmarva Peninsula is not only chicken farms. Delightful coastal towns like St. Michaels, Maryland, despite their development for tourism, are filled with flowers during the summer season.

Tapestry: sedum,
cosmos and fall foliage.
Odessa, Delaware, October.

Maryland is generally not included in the Mid-Atlantic States, but the areas we visited had more in common with this region than with states farther south. Gardens here show a bit of the formality of the southern style but have their own specific tone. The grand public display gardens of Longwood and Winterthur have had an effect on the smaller properties around them; quite sophisticated plants are available, and definite trends are apparent. Most noticeable late in the season are the ornamental grasses which have become a signature of landscape designers in the region. These useful plants are not off limits for cottage gardeners and it is nice to see them used with much more freedom than a landscape architect would allow.

Out in the rolling farmland and "hunt country" of Maryland, a fairly grand gardening style can be found, but Baltimore is an unexpected stronghold of cottage gardening. This old city has been a victim of every form of urban ill in the last few decades, but it may be climbing out of that now. Enterprising young homesteaders are rescuing run-down houses and creating communities again. Many neighborhoods have yards of just the right size for cottage gardening, and an encouraging number of new gardeners are starting to dig in, with delightful results. This is one place in the East where gardeners just starting out seem unhampered by self-conscious ideas of what a garden ought to be. Baltimore is such an eclectic mix of influences that the resulting new gardens are original, personal and wild. Another generation of cottage gardeners is starting to grow.

Topiary has always had a place in the cottage garden. These carefully crafted plant forms in the midst of the usual cottage melee of flowers may seem an anomaly, but ilex peacocks and chessmen made of yew have existed in humble English gardens from the earliest days, and in American ones as well. A mild climate conducive to the rapid growth of evergreens such as box, ilex and yew is essential, so it is not surprising that the upper and middle South abound in topiary, both in the grand, formal estate gardens and in the backyard.

Topiary; Maria Taylor.
Baltimore, Maryland,
October.

Maria Taylor and her husband moved to a small house in Baltimore in 1976. Maria, who is Scottish, was appalled by the bleak front yard: "There was nothing! I wanted to make it *alive*." It is not clear how the idea of topiary occurred to her, but it was not the inspiration of other gardens. (It was not until years later that someone told her about Ladew Gardens, a Maryland estate featuring extravagant topiary that is open to the public.) Maria Taylor simply began planting bushes and shaping them, developing her ideas and techniques as she went along.

Mrs. Taylor's garden invites participation, with neighbors dropping notes in her mailbox expressing their enjoyment and making requests. "One boy, now, he asked could I do a Cookie Monster? So that's him over there. And someone stopped by, said he had never seen a bush with boobs." She gestures toward an ample female half torso, emerging from the waist up from the ground. Since it was mid-October, all the animals had bows of black and orange.

A life-size witch leaned far out an upstairs front window.
Mrs. Taylor greeted us at the door with Halloween candy.

Most of Maria Taylor's topiaries are the traditional sculpted variety,
slowly trimmed from one or several bushes; she also has a few that
are made from wire structures covered with moss and planted with
ivy. Most of the bushes used are evergreen ilex or box, but there are
two or three lively experiments with *Euonymous alatus,* which turns a
spectacular red before dropping its leaves in the fall.

Mrs. Taylor is finding it hard to manage her own garden these days;
she is too busy making animals for others. In tubs in her crowded
backyard are the beginnings of several new dogs, bears, a running
horse. "Well, someone was just dying to have one like that, so I said
I would. And the man at the veterinary hospital wanted one for in
front of his place, and they are such nice people. . . ." None of this
is for money, of course. Says Maria Taylor: "Life is so short; you
have to make joy when you can."

The Northeast ❦ New York

Wherever you live in America is the best place to find cottage gardens. Our travels across America in the course of this book proved that anyone can descend on an arbitrarily chosen spot in this country and find cottage gardens. We did not, of course, visit every corner or even every state, but our sample was, I think, broad enough and random enough to show that cottage gardens are out there, all over. Still, you will always find the best gardens where you live. You will know all the back roads we never found, the little out-of-the-way yards that seem to explode with plants. And now, I hope, you will stop and marvel at these gardens; perhaps you will begin to share your pleasure with the people who made them. The cottage gardens around my own home in upstate New York have shaped my gardening over the past sixteen years. Today, as I drive across these hills, I am amazed to find that there are still gardens I have never seen; I'm not surprised to find that there is ever more to learn from them.

I may be trying to apologize for singling out New York in a separate chapter. I'm not attempting to prove that the gardens here are more wonderful than those anywhere else; these are simply the gardens I know best. I think in many ways they are typical of cottage gardens in many parts of America, but these gardens we could visit and photograph at their peak—something we couldn't always arrange on a three-day sprint around a region we had never seen. And these are the gardens that first inspired this book.

It may be hard, when you look at the photographs, to remember that New York has an exceedingly difficult climate for gardening. I am speaking now of upstate New York. The mild and overinhabited coastal parts of the state are, realistically, part of the Mid-Atlantic region; upstate New York is almost a region of its own, where the rocky hills and frigid temperatures of New England stretch out into the expansive space and rural life of the Midwest. The long, intense winter is like that of northern Vermont or Maine; the summer is brief, lush, cool and well watered.

Lupines. Jenny Redman.
Schoharie, New York, June.

Jenny Redman's array.
Schoharie, New York, June.

Because the growing season is so short and temperate, everything seems to bloom at once, trying to squeeze four or five months of growth into ninety days, which is frequently the period without frost. The soil in many places also has much in common with New England—the familiar and discouraging combination of acid clay and rocks. The spaciousness of the landscape, however, is very different here from New England. The hills are heavily wooded, but long, open valleys spread out between them, lined with broad pastures and fields. Views provided by the rolling landscape extend in every direction from almost any property. The life here is still, however unsuccessfully, predominantly agricultural. The economy has been straitened for decades, and land prices are only now beginning to inch up; they are still a decimal place removed from those in prosperous adjoining states and the more southerly New York counties. Acreage is a luxury of even the poorest homestead. Even the small white-and-green villages have surprisingly ample yards, seldom enclosed, which seem to wander out into the nearby fields.

The general planting style of upper New York is similar to that of the Midwest: Large clumps of a few kinds of old-fashioned flowers are scattered in a casual and undefined way around the yard. The similarity is surprising because the conditions which might have prompted this leisurely design in the Midwest are very different in New York. In the Midwest the rich topsoil makes it possible to plop a plant down anywhere with little soil preparation. Upstate the soil is so unyielding that only the most vigorous undertake to create an entire bed; it is easier for most just to dig one big hole at a time and stick a peony in it. In many parts of America, watering considerations compress garden space, but here, because of usually abundant rainfall, the gardens are not confined to the range of sprinkler or hose.

Hollyhocks and silos.
Nellie Gordon.
Lawyersville, New York, July.

The classic perennials which make up the backbone of the Midwest gardens are the same in New York: spring bulbs, iris, peonies, poppies, the wide assortment of dianthus, midsummer lilies, yarrow, rudbeckia, phlox, golden glow, fading into the fleeting autumn with sedum, artemisia and the gorgeous native asters. But because of the cool summer, New York can add a few spectacular early-summer species: lupines, which may be better here than anywhere in the country; primroses, which carry spring into July; delphiniums that can rival those grown in the Pacific Northwest.

Hardy perennials are the outstanding plants of the New York cottage garden, but they don't stand alone. Many of the warm-climate annuals need a longer season than they get here; this year if your marigolds and tomatoes were set out on Memorial Day, they got frostbitten the second week in June. But many hardy annuals and biennials self-sow and always make an appearance: opium poppies, calendula, cleome, cosmos, hollyhocks, foxgloves, hesperis and lunaria. Most of these are gratifyingly indifferent to soil conditions and naturalize into nongarden areas, gaily uniting the compost pile and the driveway with the garden. There are attractive wildflowers—or weeds, depending on your bias—that also make their way into the garden whether you want them or not: Queen Anne's lace, musk mallow, pearly everlasting. This kind of casual colonization is less often seen in the Midwest, where agriculture has disciplined the landscape, or in New England, where boundaries are more strictly enforced. There are also more choice and difficult native plants that gardeners here use to fill out their yards: trillium, jack-in-the-pulpit, ferns and mertensia for shade; *Lobelia cardinalis* and *Lychnis flos-cuculi* for damp spots; statuesque wild angelica if you have the space.

June splendor: poppies,

lupines, polymonium, chives,

Helen Gurian. Cooperstown, New York.

Roses have a hard time in this climate, although some gardeners labor to pull them through the winter. The most successful are the old shrub forms like the early Harison's yellow, a great old garden plant. Shrubs of other kinds are limited, too, by the winter, but mock orange, shrub honeysuckle and lilac are more than enough for a small yard, with hydrangeas for late-autumn bloom. Clematis is the most widely used and successful vine.

This may sound like quite a limited palette, but the gardens of New York prove that you don't need enormous plant diversity for an outstanding garden. The perennials that do well here get very big and are usually grown in large clumps; this gives a feeling of permanence to the yard. The itinerant annuals and wildflowers, when given a free hand, add grace and nonchalance. Like midwesterners, the gardeners here often grow many varieties and great numbers of a plant that does well in the climate—hundreds of hybrid iris or phlox, for example.

The cottage gardeners in my area are not necessarily sophisticated but are knowledgeable about their plants and adventurous in their selection. Local greenhouses and small nurseries frequently offer unexpected delights among the flats of petunias and geraniums: *Verbascum phoeniceum; Salvia superba; Campanula glomerata* (I saw the last carpeting an entire yard in Binghamton). The area around Ithaca, New York, because of the pervasive effect of Cornell University, is closer to the leading edge of horticulture, and it is easy to understand the presence of very well-educated plant sellers experimenting with unusual plants. My own locale, however, is out of touch about many things, so it is harder to guess why we're so lucky, except that many horticultural businesses are small and personal enough to respond to the interest of a growing number of eager gardeners.

Red maple and
iris 'Stepping Out.'
Schoharie, New York, June.

And the number of gardeners *is* growing, here and in most of the states we visited. It is not always easy to make a garden in this country, with its harsh and wildly varying climates, uncertain rainfall and difficult soils, but there are also assets that compensate: magnificent landscapes; astonishing wildflowers. In the midst of a more and more complicated society, the gardener tries to make some of that natural beauty a part of his home, a part of her life. It takes originality, energy and love. The result is the American cottage garden.

Joe Ryan showed up some years ago at my house, driving his ancient station wagon, his equally ancient but lively little French poodle under his arm. "I read in the paper you had a rock garden here," he said as he introduced himself. His own garden had suffered the last few years while he nursed his wife; now, after her death, he wanted to get started again. As he walked around, surveying the plants, his wide-ranging knowledge was unmistakable. He spotted the twisted hazel tree and chortled, "Oh, *Corylus* 'Contorta.' I never was taken in by that." He recognized *Iris pseudacorus* in a glance, even out of bloom and kindly corrected my pronunciation of it. He greeted *Allium moly* as an old friend, compared some primula species with hybrids he had grown, identified a bearded iris whose name I had never known. He admired my Siberian iris. "You ought to have that one 'Foretell,'" he suggested. A few weeks later I found a neatly labeled plant by that name in a coffee tin by my back door. I returned his visit, of course, and it was his garden that first made me think about cottage gardens.

Joe Ryan;
named varieties.
Cooperstown, New York, June.

His cottage is a trailer, his yard a tiny plot fitfully enclosed with mis-
cellaneous bits of fencing; beyond the fence the valley spreads out for
untouched miles to the low hills on either side. In a small space Joe
Ryan has made a garden you can move through, one that encloses
you in a world of diversity that is not exhausted even after many
visits. Little paths dive between interesting trees he has started
from seed; island beds present an incredible assortment of plant
life from every direction. Joe likes the old garden plants: rangy and
aromatic sweet cicely; an elegant dictamnus; a big patch of the
unusual fennel-leaf peony, which I coveted. (I found a piece of that
by my doorstep last year.) I brought him a hop plant, which he had
wanted to try; it is doing better than mine. Joe also travels to special
sales for exotic iris, day lily and rhododendron hybrids. Against one

shed the different varieties of iris are so densely planted that he has written their names on the white siding. ''Look at that 'Beverly Sills' there,'' said Joe with delight. ''I spent forty dollars for a piece of that. I said to myself, that's what the money's for, after all.''

Although his health at eighty-two wasn't too good this past spring, the beds were perfectly weeded, and he had a bunch of seedlings he wanted to try. He has been helping a friend resurrect an old rock garden and is still making the rounds of the iris sales. I brought him some new primulas and a sedum; he dug up a clump of *Iris graminea* for me. That's what a cottage garden is for, after all.

Classic Cottage Flowers

*F*ew gardens rely as utterly on flowers as does a cottage garden. In grander gardens, design or structure may have a dominant role; vistas or promenades play a part; permanent plantings of trees and shrubs are important. But in a small yard there is little room for any of that, and what a cottage gardener really wants is color and fragrance and something blooming all the time. So it is natural that flowers make the cottage garden.

As we traveled across America in the earlier chapters, you may have been dazzled by the assortment of species in the photographs. In the regional chapters I tried to point out interesting or unusual plants native to a region, as well as those that might be most characteristic of gardens throughout one area. But now let's look at the flowers that characterize the American cottage garden overall and see how they differ from the general idea of appropriate cottage garden plants.

The earliest cottage garden plants were those that were easily available, easily grown and useful. Today availability is no longer such a limiting factor; seed and bulb catalogs seek out anyone who has ever bought a trowel and provide gardeners anywhere in the country with an incredible menu of possible plants. But the diverse climates of this country have their own strict form of censorship; you may be able to *buy* anything, but it remains to be seen if you can grow it. So many cottage gardeners are likely to start with plants available from local sources. Since the 1950's, commercial sources provided little variety: half-hardy annuals like petunias and marigolds predominated, but a few old-fashioned perennials—peonies, bleeding heart, phlox—could usually be found by the persistent plant hunter. This has changed dramatically in the past decade. Now local sources offer a much wider variety of plants, especially perennials. In some parts of the country you can find for sale at small local nurseries species almost unknown to commerce a few years ago.

Hollyhocks.
East Worcester,
New York, July.

Roses.

Edmond L. Emery.

Clinton, Connecticut, July.

Another way of acquiring plants that do well in a region is to get them from gardeners already growing them. Plant sharing has always played a big part in the life of the cottage gardener. In small English villages where cottages were close together, it was easy to hand plants back and forth across the fence. In America the much greater distances make this more difficult, but the practice still goes on. One notable phenomenon is the way one garden will set off two or three others in the same neighborhood. You could be riding around for hours without seeing a flower, then suddenly find several lively gardens all in one block. This usually starts with one avid gardener who begins sharing ''slips'' or cuttings with her neighbor; then someone across the street takes notice, and the first two start passing plants on to him. In a small yard there are always surplus plants to give away. This is one reason why the most popular cottage garden plants are those easily propagated; it is also the reason why one variety of a species will suddenly appear over and over in one area.

In America an ''easy'' plant is not necessarily one that requires little care; it usually means a plant that will survive. It goes without saying that many plants that were easy and accommodating in English gardens can be anything but happy in American ones. Primroses, for example, have been a characteristic cottage plant in England since at least the sixteenth century; in America there are only a few areas where primroses will survive with any reliability, and even in those regions they don't seem to inspire the kind of affection they get in Britain. Hollyhocks, in contrast, are one of the classics abroad as well as in any part of America; I would dare to say they are better loved here and are certainly grown in America with a freer hand.

The overall first impression one gets from a cottage garden is a combination of profusion and diversity; the profusion is definitely one aspect, but the diversity comes and goes, dictated by region and season. Pacific Coast gardens, for example, are like English models in the incredible range of plants, many of which stay in bloom for a long season.

Rose and camellia.
Janie Porter. Ashland,
Mississippi, May.

In most of the rest of our country, seasons of bloom are shorter and more definite, and the range of species that will survive is more limited. There are also more gardens here that favor spectacular plantings of just one or two species in bloom at one time—yards completely filled with only iris, or dahlias, or gladiolus, as we have seen.

Gardening books are much given to list making; there are volumes that offer their definitive lineups of the "right" cottage plants. This is interesting and perhaps useful when we are talking about a distant historical period, but anyone who has spent time visiting cottage gardens must be struck by its irrelevance. Cottage gardeners grow what they want to grow. Particularly in America, these gardens are not made as historical re-creations; they do not follow a tradition but make one up as they go along. What is interesting to discover is that in spite of this independence and in spite of the great differences of climate from one state to the next, there are some plants that are universal favorites of cottage gardeners all across America.

Roses must top the list of cottage garden favorites in any country or any region of America except the most northern. It doesn't matter how much effort is involved—and in most parts of America, that effort is considerable. Cottage gardeners don't care. If there is any plant that is close to universal in the gardens of this country, it is the hybrid tea rose. Hybrid tea roses are best loved and most useful in the South, where they will produce blooms from April to November. They are not beautiful plants, but they usually look better in the confines of a crowded garden where other plants can hide their gawky shapes. Hybrid tea roses are susceptible to all manner of insects and diseases, but this does not deter their fans. The real foe of this rose is cold—Zone 5 is pretty much the northern limit, and even there, protection is important. But gardeners in the North are not completely without rose resources. Old-fashioned shrub roses like Father Hugo's rose or Harison's yellow are scattered in yards far into the North.

Peonies.
Kokomo, Indiana, June.

Species roses like the Apothecary's rose, *Rosa gallica officinalis,* or *R. rugosa* are extremely rugged. There are climbing or "pillar" roses from the turn of the century to loop over gates or hang from arbors in all climates.

The iris, like the rose, has the advantage of a wide range of species to guarantee its success in any climate. Appropriately named for the goddess of the rainbow, the iris appears in an astonishing assortment of colors, sizes and shapes. It is a rare garden in America that does not have at least one kind of iris. *Iris x germanica,* the tall bearded German iris, is the best known of the family. Graceful, imposing, resplendent in virtually every color and two-tone variations, this is an irresistible plant. Oddly, it is seldom mentioned as an English cottage flower, but even if it were, there is no doubt that it is the Americans who have made the iris what it is today. Our climate, with its brilliant sunshine and baking heat to ripen the corms, simply suits this plant. The German iris is only part of the story. There are native irises widely used in American gardens: *I. fulva; I. brevicaulis; I. versicolor. Iris spuria* is not a native but is right at home in unlikely places like Texas. Siberian iris are as hardy as their name implies and are almost foolproof.

Although the hollyhock is only one species, it probably has as wide a distribution in America as the far-flung iris. Long a European favorite, this towering beauty can really show off in the more ample yards of this country. The hollyhock hovers somewhere between a biennial

Poppies and iris.
Clearfield, Pennsylvania, May.

and a perennial; it is one of those plants that does best by self-sowing and making its own patch. (One gardener in my area, an elderly lawyer in Lawyersville, New York, grows nothing but hollyhocks and has a field of them between her house and barn.)

Biennials that self-sow easily, like the hollyhock, often make a place for themselves in the cottage garden. Foxgloves, sweet rocket (hesperis) and lunaria, the money plant, are three favorites in cooler climates of the United States. All three will reproduce abundantly and effortlessly and will come up almost anywhere; they are particularly useful for shady corners where many perennials won't grow. All bloom early, before most perennials get started, and have a long season in places where summer heat comes late.

The peony is not a universally grown plant in America because it will not survive in warm climates that don't provide a period of dormancy. But in the extensive parts of America where it is grown, it is a dominant garden presence. This gorgeous flower is rarely mentioned in books on the English cottage garden, in part because it was introduced too late in the nineteenth century to be a true early English favorite but also, I suspect, because it is simply too big for small English plots. Not only is it large, but it is virtually immovable once it is established. In America it provides a few weeks of glory all across the northern section of the country. Peonies may take up too much space for their brief moment of bloom, but they are utterly carefree and will outlive any gardener who plants them.

Tulips and dogwood.
Natchez, Mississippi, March.

Poppies join with peonies and iris in creating the most typical spring garden pictures in America. The perennial Oriental poppies are big, sprawling plants best kept outside a small garden but are vibrant additions to a larger yard. They are hardy anywhere and all but ineradicable. The annual Shirley poppies, developed from the European corn poppy, are cottage favorites in England and America; they have a very different character from their enormous perennial relatives. These slender, graceful plants self-sow everywhere and occupy little space. They usually seem to grow best in the center of the garden path, but they are so charming, with their nodding heads and vivid shades of pink, red and orange, that it is a stern gardener who insists on pulling them out. These do best in a cool climate, but there is one surprising poppy at home with both heat or cold. When I first began looking at gardens around my home in upstate New York, I was puzzled by the prevalence of a poppy with a gray-green, glaucous foliage and fat, rounded seedpods. Wasn't this the opium poppy, that symbol of death and addiction from the Far East? Well, it is, in fact, although no cottage gardeners seem to know or care. Seed is passed from one gardener to another, the plant self-sows like wild, and this poppy is cheerfully blooming, its ominous reputation unknown, in every corner of this country.

Long before the peonies and poppies are aboveground, the garden starts to bloom with the familiar array of spring bulbs: snowdrops; crocuses; daffodils; tulips. All these are cottage garden classics and grow everywhere in the United States with one exception: Tulips do badly in California and parts of the South where they can't go dormant. The small early bulbs fit in any odd corners of the garden; narcissus, in contrast, make sizable clumps with copious foliage in a few years, so are often seen in naturalized plantings outside the yard. Tulips have a more formal look and frequently inspire plantings of similar formality. But the bulb season is scarcely begun with spring.

Phlox and golden glow.
Near Skowhegan, Maine, August.

Alliums are unexpectedly popular in all areas through the summer; because of the great assortment of species, there are many that do well in every climate. Some alliums are edible garden staples, like chives, leeks and onions, but the ornamental varieties have many supporters. Gardeners in the South and Southwest grow some bulb flowers northern gardeners look at as impossibly exotic: tuberose; crinum; lycoris. Possibly the most striking of these are the amaryllis species (most of these are, botanically speaking, *Hippeastrum* but are seldom called that). It doesn't seem possible that these magnificent flowers could simply spring up in humble, disheveled yards, but they do, shedding glory in the most unlikely places.

The lily is a universally loved summer bulb plant. The Madonna lily is a signature cottage flower in England, and it is common in American gardens as well, but there are so many other lilies available these days that gardeners seldom limit their selection to *Lilium candidum*. The vivid orange tiger lily, seen on page 116, is far more common, often making big stands in old gardens.

We shouldn't overlook the gladiolus among the bulb selection. Gardeners and nongardeners have strong feelings about this flower, which is both enormously popular and much hated. It is cheap, reliable, colorful and very productive; it almost always looks peculiar coming out of the ground, and it reminds people of funerals. I'm not going to take sides. It is in gardens everywhere.

Cottage gardens have always been noted for their use of native plants. In America natives contribute some of the most original effects in the cottage garden. Some species are extremely local in distribution and are difficult to grow in other regions, but there are others that are found in almost all parts of the country. Phlox is seldom

Yucca and climbing roses.
Manchester-by-the-Sea,
Massachusetts, July.

mentioned in English books, but this versatile genus opens and closes the season in American yards. Moss pink (actually *Phlox subulata*) makes broad swaths of bright color in early spring and is abhorred by many as a rock garden cliché; in spite of that, it is extremely popular. The tall garden phlox, *P. paniculata*, starts blooming in July and persists for months. There are glorious hybrids of these species (although they all tend to return to magenta if left to self-sow), and they quickly make huge clumps, so that many cottage gardens seem made up of nothing but phlox and golden glow by late August.

The yucca is a statuesque American native with a formidable rosette of stiff, swordlike leaves (hence the nicknames Spanish bayonet or Adam's needle) and a tall plume of white flowers in midsummer. It looks like a cliché of the landscape of the American West, and several species do hail from there; but you are just as likely to find it punctuating lawns in New Jersey or on the sands of Cape Cod. *Yucca filamentosa*, the species with the greatest tolerance of cold and wet ground, may have the widest distribution of any native garden plant in the United States.

Golden glow (*Rudbeckia laciniata* 'Hortensia') is another American species that has become a universal fixture. It is lanky, invasive and prone to flop over just as it comes into bloom. It's hard to know how many gardeners grow it because they like it and how many have it because they can't get rid of it. It is wonderfully prolific and has a long season of shining yellow bloom.

Rudbeckia, ratibida, coreopsis, helianthus, gaillardia, echinacea— these are all American stalwarts from the vast daisy family, the Compositae. Without them the American cottage garden would be meager indeed. All these are perennial members of the clan, but there are annual composites, too, that we wouldn't want to be without. Cosmos and zinnias are both Mexican in origin but still are very much at home anywhere else on the continent.

Annuals: bells of Ireland,
celosia, corn, sunflowers.
Jessica and Dean Smith.
Billings, Montana, August.

In general, annuals seem to have a more prominent place in American gardens than in English ones; much of this is determined by climate. Highly visible annuals like African marigolds, petunias, zinnias or giant sunflowers do best in limitless sunshine and dry weather, so they are natural choices for the American summer. Larkspur probably has the widest American distribution of any single annual; it is an English cottage classic and carries the tradition across the United States.

What about woody plants? However small the yard, there is usually enough room for a few shrubs. In the Deep South and in California shrubs are actually the dominating garden feature; in California, especially, there is a great range of woody plants available that the rest of the country has never seen. Woody plants in general are more limited in their range, more susceptible to winter damage or more in need of a dormant period. For that reason there are few shrubs that can be found all over. In the South, azaleas and camellias are dominant; osmanthus (tea olive), gardenia, hibiscus, buddleia, crape myrtle and hydrangea (*Hydrangea macrophylla*, the pink and blue ones) fill the ranks. In the North, lilac, bridal wreath, shrub honeysuckle and the hardy hydrangeas, *H. arborescens* and *H. paniculata*, are most commonly seen.

Somewhere between perennials and shrubs, somewhere between the earth and the air, are the vines. There are few things that can make a dull house look more like a quaint cottage than a drapery of climbing roses or clematis. Vines are invaluable in a small yard. They can utilize vertical growing space, emerging from a few modest stems to cover an entire pergola or the wall of the garage.

They also provide a garden overhead, drooping down from arbors above. In areas where it can survive, bougainvillea makes an arresting display for many months. This shrubby vine is often too big for a small garden and is best kept to the outskirts of the property. Wisteria may be the most characteristic southern vine; jasmine is widely grown but has a less overpowering visual effect, although its perfume is intoxicating. In the North clematis is queen, first the large-flow-

Bougainvillea.
Key Largo, Florida, August.

ered species like *Jackmanii,* followed in late summer by frothy native *Clematis virginiana,* which is lovely in bloom but even more spectacular later, when it is covered with its masses of silvery, silky seed heads. There are many native clematis species, and quite a few are hardy both north and south. The most-mentioned English cottage vine is woodbine, or honeysuckle. In America it is either not hardy, in the North, or so wildly invasive that one would have to be crazy to put it in a small yard. It is still much loved but enjoyed best in the wild.

Looking over this limited list, all I notice are the plants I left out: graceful aquilegia, which has native species throughout our country and which seems to bloom from April to August; sturdy sweet william, America's favorite member of the rich *Dianthus* genus; monarda, our spectacular crimson native, loved by bees and hummingbirds. You may find a few of these plants in classic English cottage gardens, or in books about them, but the majority mentioned above are most at home in this country. They suit our landscapes and our climates, and they are the plants best loved by our gardeners. They do not begin to describe the diversity of the gardens around us, but they provide us with an outline of what is common to many. For new gardeners in this country, these plants can provide an easy introduction to the pleasures of growing flowers, just one of the many ways we can learn from the American cottage garden.

Wisteria.
Natchez, Mississippi, March.

Garden Architecture and Garden Ornaments

There is more to a garden than the plants. In a cottage garden it is true that flowers are the focus, but this does not eliminate the need or the desire to go beyond the world of growing things. In any garden there are design elements which order the space and direct movement around and through the flowers; there are architectural or structural devices which show us where to pause, where to sit, where to look. The small size of most cottage gardens makes a great deal of architecture unnecessary, but any garden larger than a row of zinnias has some need of order. The gardens you have seen in some of these pictures may seem impossibly disordered, but even the most jumbled relies on a few basic elements to hold it together: a fence; a path; a gate; an edge. Somewhat more elaborate devices include arbors and trellises, benches and other forms of outdoor seating, pools and fountains, walls and rocks. All these structural elements which give form and direction to a planting, those things which make a plot of flowers into a garden, we will look at under the title of garden architecture.

It is probably unnecessary to add that few of the gardeners represented in this book think of anything in terms of garden architecture. Some cottage gardeners are more conscious than others of garden design, but for most, design exists chiefly in terms of problem solving: how to get from here to there; how to hide this or get around that. In a cottage garden the design never exists for its own sake; rather, it develops from the landscape, the flowers and the spirit of the garden.

One of the first concerns of most gardeners is defining the space of the garden. Enclosed yards are rare in most parts of America. They exist in cities, and they can be found with some frequency in small towns of New England, but in most parts of this country, "Don't fence me in" seems to be the slogan. Yards flow into one another and into the vast surrounding landscape with a nonchalance that Europeans find alarming.

Echinops and lattice.
Cobleskill, New York, July.

The timeless trellis.
Portlandville,
New York, July.

The white-picketed plots of New England offer a setting ready-made for a garden. But in the rest of the United States the enclosing elements may be no more substantial than the edges of the property—driveways, sidewalks, curbs—over and around which the flowers sway. Where fences do exist, they are often defensive, strong but not particularly pretty deterrents to the numerous forms of plant-loving wildlife America still has to offer. In Colorado or Wyoming you can find delightful plantings cowering behind eight feet of chain link, but that is preferable to a moose on your doorstep. Often a fence or wall won't enclose a garden but will make a backdrop for one section of planting; it is not surprising to find plantings along a fence where the flowers have colonized so freely on either side that you can no longer tell what is being closed in from what is closed out. There are marked regional trends in fences: In the Deep South, the delicate tracery of wrought iron is standard; this is also surprisingly common in parts of the Midwest. Freestanding dry walls or planted retaining walls are part of the Northeast and Northwest garden landscape. Post-and-rail extends from the Mid-Atlantic States down through the South. The picket fence has long been popular everywhere and is now in danger of being a garden fad. In spite of that, it will always be a graceful and effective garden element. In English and European cottage gardens, hedges are commonly used to close off the yard; this is remarkably rare in America.

Weeding along the path. Roy Patton. Ojai, California, February.

Swing and pot birdhouse,
Elsie Weiddenhoff.
Huntington, Indiana, May.

The American garden may dispense with a fence, but a path, however informal, is essential. This is often what distinguishes a garden from a mere plot of flowers. Practically speaking, a path gives greater access to beds for weeding and watering; beyond that, the path is the means by which the gardener shows us how to move through his garden and how to look at it. Once we are moving among the plants, other design features come into play. The path may go under an arbor, so climbing plants may be enjoyed from below. Benches along a path indicate a particular spot to be savored. Steps up or down mark a pause and a change of perspective. All this, remember, can take place in a very small area, although the same effects work on a larger scale as well. Breaking up a small garden and allowing movement through it are ways of increasing the sense of space. The paths themselves can consist of almost anything: gravel, grass, concrete slabs, plastic mulch, old newspapers or bare earth.

America loves lattice. Whether as part of a trellis, as a plant support against a building or as a freestanding openwork wall in the garden, lattice is one of the most commonly found garden accents. Latticework provides a light background for some sections of planting without interfering with the open nature of the garden. It can create a support for vines or climbers. It can frame a bench or swing. Despite its airy structure, lattice is surprisingly durable; often the trellises of another age persist to frame the flowers of the present. But today's gardener may have his own ideas of garden design, and it is common in the gardens of old houses to find the trellises wandering in one direction while the garden takes off in another.

Benches, seats, swings—the gardener may never have a chance to use them, but they form a major focus of many gardens. A southern garden without a place to sit or recline is unthinkable; this region has the widest repertoire of outdoor furniture in every style. Californians, who practically live outside year-round, frequently shape their plantings with that in mind. Italian and Latin gardeners, no matter where they live, manage to find space for a table and chairs. A bench or lawn chair may seem an extremely simple element in the garden, but it is seldom placed without some care.

Container gardening.

Mr. and Mrs. Schramm.

Laguna Beach, California, February.

A seat defines space around it and provides a different way of seeing the garden. Gardeners realize this intuitively and respond by enhancing the view from the seats, by creating islands of space or by drawing in more intimate plantings around them.

In some regions the geography of the area dictates elements of garden design. In Seattle or San Francisco, for example, the rocky vertical yards have resulted in a very consistent form of hanging garden. Rocks always have a decisive effect on gardens that have them; it is usually easier to use them than to get rid of them, so gardeners in rocky parts of the United States find themselves building terraces or retaining walls simply in an effort to use up the rock piles around the property. Rocks are not always functional in a cottage garden; frequently they are painted and used as decorative accents. Beatrice Wyatt's garden in Ventura, California (pages 64–65), may be the last word on the painted rock, but there are many smaller, less elaborate yards where edges are highlighted by a bright white or pink circle of stones.

Where the soil is nothing *but* rocks, gardens can be created in planters above the ground. Freestanding containers for plants are useful features for improving design and horticulture at the same time. Containers can isolate difficult-to-grow species, providing special soil, improved drainage or better exposure than other beds in the garden. As I mention in the California chapter, containers enable gardeners with limited space to utilize nongarden areas such as steps, patios and sidewalks. Plants in pots above the ground create a visual accent; also, some plants need to be isolated from the hurly-burly of the usual cottage-style planting. A great many gardeners simply bring out into the yard all the semitropical plants they have enjoyed indoors through the winter; this is especially true of Hispanic or Italian gardeners, who have a particular love of growing and training plants in pots.

Basket planters.
San Antonio, Texas, April.

The contrast between the tropical indoor material and the temperate-zone outdoor garden plants can be startling or chaotic, but the pots isolate the exotics and maintain an interesting visual balance. The pots themselves are an additional decorative feature, since few cottage gardeners are content with mere terra-cotta. Plants can be found sprouting in everything from a coffeepot or milk crate to a refrigerator or bathtub. Boats are favored as planters in coastal regions. In San Antonio, Texas, enormous concrete baskets adorn the lawns all over town. Truck tires, painted or not, are extremely popular; on an asphalt yard in Salt Lake City a garden is grown completely in abandoned tires. There is one method of cutting the rubber which makes the top flare; when the tire is placed on top of the metal rim, the whole thing becomes an impromptu urn.

Water is always a desirable garden element in any form. A natural stream or pond is a blessing, and there are few gardens too small to have a tiny decorative pool of some sort. Besides making a focal point, water adds to the range of plants that can be grown by providing an area with damp soil. The reflective value of the water is another asset, doubling the beauty of flowers grown around it. Even a birdbath can bring a patch of sky down into the garden.

When we talk of birdbaths and planters made from boats, we begin to edge away from what might be called garden architecture. Besides the landscape features that give a garden form, there are often non-flower elements that have no purpose other than decoration.

Birdbath.
Arthur Wallace.
Jonesboro, Arkansas, May.

This is how we might define garden ornament. Architectural and structural features are usually essential to the form of the garden, and they develop from the shape and surroundings of the property. Garden ornaments are seldom essential to anything, and they usually develop from little more than the whim of the gardener. But these ornaments do contribute to the spirit and character of the garden by expressing some aspect of its creator. Ornaments make a garden personal, and they are an outstanding characteristic of the American cottage garden.

At the words "garden ornament," two images immediately come to mind: religious statues and pink flamingos. There is no doubt that there are a lot of both in the yards of America, and we may be accused of snobbishly ignoring them in these photographs. But the fact is that the flamingos and religious icons often exist *instead of* a garden rather than in one. You are more likely to see pink flamingos in a bare yard of grass and foundation plantings than in one filled with flowers. Grottoes and statues of the Virgin may have little plantings or pots clustered around them, but it is not common to find them in the midst of a wildly planted garden. There are noticeable regional trends in religious display. In New Orleans it seems as if half the yards have grottoes or statues, but these seldom coincide with the most exuberant plantings. In Southern California Hispanic gardeners provide most displays of a religious nature; in New England there is scarcely a Virgin to be seen.

Birdhouse and scarecrow.
Jessica and Dean Smith.
Billings, Montana, August.

In the mid-South we drove for days without seeing anything ornamental; then suddenly in the middle of Kentucky we went through a
town with an icon on every lawn. Many of the gardeners we met
expressed strong and very open religious feelings, and the great
majority are regular churchgoers, but for most of our cottage gardeners the act of gardening and the flowers that result are their state-
ment of faith. A mere statue would be beside the point.

Birdhouses, on the other hand, are everywhere in the garden, in all
parts of the country. Even gardens with scarecrows also provide
houses and feeders to lure birds into the yard. There is a strong sym-
biotic connection between bird and gardener, and it is a rare garden
that doesn't provide some encouragement for feathered friends. The
variety of birdhouses is incredible; most are handmade by the gardener out of anything available: a broken flowerpot and a slab of
wood; old bleach bottles; dried gourds; scraps of twine, twig and
cornhusks. In size they range from tiny bluebird bungalows to the
grand palaces made for martins in the South, luxury apartment
buildings often more elaborate than the houses of the gardeners. The
houses in themselves are delightful; they are all the more valuable for
bringing another kind of life into the garden.

Other forms of garden ornamentation are more diverse. Some ornaments—the whirlybirds, for example—make a claim of being functional. These are wooden birds (usually ducks, but I bought a roadrunner for myself this summer) with wings that spin around when the wind blows. It is explained by those who buy and sell these birds that moles are alarmed by the vibrations of the spinning and will leave the area. This seems to have no basis in fact, but that has not discouraged the thousands of gardeners who use the whirlybirds, often in great flocks, to adorn their yards.

Gardeners like to know which way the wind blows. Other ornaments designed to catch the breezes are chimes of glass, metal, shells or bone; weather vanes of every description; and flags. There is no question that the gardeners of America love Old Glory and give it a prominent place (or places) in their yards. Although none of our garden visits were made on major patriotic holidays, the Stars and Stripes greeted us wherever we went. Besides the flag itself, there were plantings made to replicate it or special beds all in red, white and blue.

Some garden ornaments are larger in scale and would almost count as garden architecture if they had any conceivable purpose. Perhaps a few of the many wishing wells did once work, but now most of them are so bedecked with flowers it is hard even to get to them, much less draw water. And how can one explain the presence of miniature windmills? These are by no means rare. Some, found not surprisingly in the yards of Dutch gardeners, are perfectly scaled-down old Holland mills. Others are the stilty and angular Great Plains variety. Pet oil rigs are another all-American version of the same idea.

There is no point in trying to *explain* any of these ornaments. They demonstrate the same lively humor and eccentricity that we have seen everywhere in American cottage gardens, the same originality that makes every one of these gardens different.

Easter-egg tree.
Natchez, Mississippi, March.

The ornaments are a forceful reminder that these gardens are the results of the imagination and love of the people who make them, people who are not limited by what others expect. There are many inescapable limits in the lives of American cottage gardeners: They usually have little space; they often have a fixed income, or very little income at all; they are often advanced in years and unable physically to accomplish all that they would like. But they still are free to do what they want with their yards, and through their gardens these individuals present their ideas and beliefs in every season.

We should mention, in closing, the seasonal forms of garden ornament. Since the holidays most commonly celebrated with outdoor decoration—Christmas, Easter and Halloween—don't fall during the peak gardening season, much of this kind of ornamentation seems like a way of drawing out the pleasure of gardening before and after the flowers are gone. Easter egg trees appear with the early daffodils; at Halloween figures of ghosts and witches, pumpkins and cornstalks join late chrysanthemums in braving the frost. Reindeer, Santa, crèche scenes and millions of lights fill the empty yards through December and January, when gardeners can barely remember what their summer blossoms looked like. But by moving their celebrations outdoors, American gardeners keep that feeling of being in their yards in spite of the long winter, the late spring, the early freeze. So our cottage gardeners arrange light bulbs instead of tulip bulbs and set up the Wise Men where the peonies will bloom in May. When they take down Santa's reindeer in January, it is almost time to start the first seeds indoors. Another year in the cottage garden has begun.

Afterword

Eve Sonneman and I set out to make a book about gardening in America. I hope the result goes beyond that and is more than a simple record of who grows what where. We wanted to show just how diverse and individual gardening can be, how inventive and brave Americans are in dealing with the difficulties of their climates. But that still meant leaving out a great deal. For example, we couldn't begin to tell all of our adventures simply in finding these gardens. As you probably noticed, these are not the kinds of gardens that would be included on a garden club tour or featured in a national magazine. Many are unnoticed even by close neighbors. In a few areas garden club members were helpful with suggestions. In other places we relied on family, friends, friends of friends and often people we picked and called up almost at random. When all else failed, we simply drove out across the countryside, hoping a cottage garden would throw itself in our path. Surprisingly often, it did. It is probably clear from the pictures that almost none of the gardeners knew in advance that we were coming, so there was no special "primping" for the photographs. These gardens look just as they would if you stopped to visit them tomorrow.

What was most wonderful to discover was the unfailing generosity and friendliness of the American people. It may be true that gardeners as a breed are the nicest people in the world; American gardeners surpass any definition of nice. We knocked on the doors of hundreds of complete strangers in every part of this land and were not greeted with one suspicious question, one shotgun or one snarling dog. We were offered plants, meals, places to stay and guided tours of the neighborhood by gardeners we had talked to for five minutes. No matter how little they had, they were ready to share it with two women who had appeared without warning on their doorsteps.

We knew when we started that we wouldn't be able to include every state. It seemed more interesting to have several images of one garden, and several gardens in one state, than just one shot of many, so we tried to select representative areas in all the major climate zones of the country. It is unfortunate that some states had to be left out, but perhaps sometime in the next few years we will be persuaded to take to the road again.

Our book is an appreciation of the creativity of American cottage gardeners and is our thank-you to them for their efforts. We would also like to thank the many people who helped us who are not gardeners or who don't have the kind of garden we were seeking. Some of these are relatives or old friends; many were people who became friends through their generous aid to this book. Even if they were not cottage gardeners, they had a special knack for finding just the kind of garden we wanted. American cottage gardens exist in backyards all over our country; thanks to the people listed below, we were able to find them, share them, photograph them and make them known to everyone.

In Ojai, California, my sister Barbara and her husband, Ted Cartee, and Alasdair Coyne; in Santa Barbara, California, Sidney Baumgartner; in Texas, Jim Hyde in San Antonio, Beverly Lowery in San Marcos, John Davidson in Austin; in Baltimore, Christy Macy and Taylor Branch; Martha Baltzall in Philadelphia; Joshua Pailet in New Orleans; Eulalie Bull in Natchez; Ann Rickey and Tom Mitchell in Memphis; Gretchen Chambers and Bill Ames in Seattle; Ann Model in Cody, Wyoming; Richard Hildreth in Salt Lake City; Inez and Fred McGaughy in Ashland, Mississippi; and my parents, John and Natalie Thorpe, in New Jersey and Connecticut. Special thanks also to the three men to whom the book is dedicated: Mat thew Fraser and Harold and Sam Stults. They made it possible to go away and even better to return.

Index

Photo: Richard Duncan

Photo: Matthew Fraser

About the Author

Patricia Thorpe is a contributor to *House & Garden,* where her own garden has been featured. She is the author of *The American Weekend Garden* and *Everlastings: The Complete Book of Dried Flowers.* Ms. Thorpe lives in New York City and East Worcester, New York, with her husband and son.

About the Photographer

Eve Sonneman's photographs are a part of the collections of the Museum of Modern Art and the Centre Pompidou. Her work is represented by Leo Castelli Galleries. She recently won France's Cartier Foundation Fellowship in the Arts, and is the author of *Real Time* and coauthor, with Klaus Kertess, of *Roses Are Read.* Ms. Sonneman lives in New York City with her fiancé.

Graphic Credits

The color separations in this book were prepared by Dai Nippon, Tokyo, Japan, from original photographs by Eve Sonneman.
The text of this book was set in the film version of Bernhard by University Graphics, Inc., Atlantic Highlands, New Jersey.
The book was printed and bound by Dai Nippon, Tokyo, Japan.
Manufacturing and production were directed by Dennis E. Dwyer;
R.D. Scudellari designed and directed the graphics;
Carsten H. Fries was production editor.